# Film, In Theory

# Film, In Theory

## *The BFI Education Department and Film Culture*

Colm McAuliffe

BLOOMSBURY ACADEMIC
LONDON • NEW YORK • OXFORD • NEW DELHI • SYDNEY

BLOOMSBURY ACADEMIC
Bloomsbury Publishing Plc, 50 Bedford Square, London, WC1B 3DP, UK
Bloomsbury Publishing Inc, 1359 Broadway, New York, NY 10018, USA
Bloomsbury Publishing Ireland, 29 Earlsfort Terrace, Dublin 2, D02 AY28, Ireland

BLOOMSBURY, BLOOMSBURY ACADEMIC and the Diana logo are trademarks of Bloomsbury Publishing Plc

First published in Great Britain 2026



Cover design: Louise Dugdale



A catalogue record for this book is available from the British Library.

A catalog record for this book is available from the Library of Congress.

ISBN: HB: 978-1-8390-2633-1
ePDF: 978-1-8390-2635-5
eBook: 978-1-8390-2634-8

Typeset by Newgen KnowledgeWorks Pvt. Ltd., Chennai, India
Printed and bound in Great Britain

For product safety related questions contact productsafety@bloomsbury.com.

To find out more about our authors and books visit www.bloomsbury.com
and sign up for our newsletters.

# Contents

# Figures

# Acknowledgements

I would like to thank all the interviewees for this book who so graciously took the time to speak to me, often at great length, about their time working in and around the BFI Education Department and with *Screen* journal: Cary Bazalgette, Victor Burgin, Ed Buscombe, David Buckingham, the late Gerald Cinamon, Leslie Dick, Richard Dyer, John Ellis, Jon Halliday, Christine Geraghty, Christine Gledhill, Paul Kerr, Annette Kuhn, the late Alan Lovell, David Lusted, Colin MacArthur, Colin MacCabe, Mandy Merck, Barry Miles, Juliet Mitchell, Laura Mulvey, Richard Paterson, Griselda Pollock, Jacqueline Rose, Jonathan Rosenbaum, the late Anthony Smith, Rod Stoneman, Ian Wall, Garry Whannel and Judith Williamson. I'm sorry I didn't have room to include everyone's perspectives. I would like to add an extra thanks to Colin MacArthur, Judith Williamson, Garry Whannel and Laura Mulvey for advice and encouragement beyond the call of duty, especially when my morale was flagging. Garry Whannel also provided me with a near-full complement of *Screen* from the late 1960s through 1980 while Christine Geraghty provided me with a similar amount of *Screen Education* issues from the same time period along with other important material from her time at the BFI – this made my work so much easier.

All interview quotes are from interviews with the author unless ascribed separately in the text.

Thanks also to Nicolas Helm-Grovas and Oliver Fuke who shared thoughts and research on Peter Wollen's work, Dany Nobus who helped with tracing Lacan's translations in Britain, Mark Reid who helped me navigate the BFI's archives and Wendy Russell at the BFI Archive who provided access to crucial material. I am also hugely grateful to Phil Wickham at the excellent Bill Douglas Cinema Museum at the University of Exeter which houses a magnificent film archive where I found crucial BFI and *Screen*-related publications. Similarly, Caroline Beven was very helpful in allowing me to sit in her office and comb through the *Screen* archive at the University of Glasgow and thank you to Finn

Daniels-Yeoman for encouraging me to visit this archive. Catie Huggins at Northwestern University opened the archive especially for me to view Paddy Whannel's files and a special thank you to Mick Hayes and Clancy Potts for their wonderful hospitality in Barrington, Illinois, and Chicago, Illinois.

The Society of Authors provided a generous grant to write this book, and their Drusilla Harvey fund allowed me to visit the Paddy Whannel archive at Northwestern University.

Anna Coatman, Rebecca Barden, Rex Cleaver and Veidehi Hans were very encouraging of this project at Bloomsbury/BFI, thank you for all your hard work on this project.

Thank you to Luke Ingram and all at the Wylie Agency.

Much of the research for this book was originally conducted as part of a PhD at Birkbeck, University of London. I would like to thank Joe Brooker, my supervisor, and my external examiners Catherine Grant and Sukhdev Sandhu for continued kindness and encouragement.

Finally, I would like to thank Luke Browne, Gareth Evans, Matthew Harle, Fiona Hegarty, Ciara Lawless, Sara Lima, James Mullighan, and my family – Barry, Carol and Mary McAuliffe, and Luey Graves and Dougal – for their love and support.

# Introduction

The British Film Institute was founded in the 1930s with a singular intention: to decisively shape the social and moral attitudes of children through the advent of film.[1] The Institute's education department had a more specific role: to cultivate a sense of 'film appreciation', creating a strong filter between the messages of films perceived to be 'good' and films perceived to be 'bad'. Good films were the Ealing comedies, the works of Carol Reed, David Lean and the documentary films of Humphrey Jennings. Bad films were the crude and unrealistic representations of modern life as depicted by Hollywood narrative cinema.

By the mid-1960s, this outlook had been turned on its head. Paddy Whannel, a Scottish working-class war veteran who left school at the age of fourteen to train as a projectionist and joined the BFI Education Department in 1957, initiated a far-reaching intellectual drive to transform the department into a thoroughly modern and progressive laboratory of ideas. Whannel's mission was to create a 'film culture' which would be, at the very least, a parallel to the existing literary culture in Britain but also one which would become the new vanguard, underpinning the BFI Education Department's modernist approach to film education.

Dispensing with the privileged territories of individual taste, the department's work now reads like the beginning of a new epoch for film study: they began hosting a series of experimental seminars, showcasing readings of Hollywood films both close and wide, encompassing exciting new theories from semiology, structuralism and allowing for interconnections between cultural spheres

[1] The British Film Institute hereafter referred to as BFI.

otherwise assumed discreet. They revamped the BFI Summer Schools: in 1965, the school's star attraction was a lecture on fame by Peter Sellars and Britt Ekland, but by 1966, this was cast aside by a lecture by Peter Wollen on reading the Western through the structuralist methods of Claude Lévi-Strauss. They founded a publishing imprint, the Cinema One series, which published a remarkable range of books on topics ranging from semiotics and film to auteurist studies of contemporary filmmakers. They re-founded both SEFT, the Society for Education in Film and Television, and *Screen*, once a journal for teachers, as a comprehensively theoretical journal where forms of feminist film critique, spearheaded by Claire Johnston and Laura Mulvey, emerged in the mid-1970s. And the Education Department pioneered the inauguration of film as a serious site for study, funding lectureships in film studies across the UK.

The work of the BFI Education Department was unprecedented and film studies was transformed forever. Not only did the combination of resources and intellectually curious people at the department allow film studies to form intellectually, but film extracts were made available to schools and educational institutions and a remarkable range of study guides was made available to educators and students. The BFI Education Department was a fertile terrain for the exchange of ideas and resources, fostering interdisciplinary exchange, debate, interpretation and, as we will see, remarkable levels of rancour and antagonism. There was no other comparable institution to the BFI within the Anglophone world.

This book is about this era, primarily the 1960s and 1970s, of the BFI Education Department and *Screen* journal. It captures the origins of film as a topic for study as seen through the work of several people who worked in and around these institutions in London. While this indicates the book is entirely about film, there is a caveat: it *is* film, but primarily *in theory*. The film captured by the period covered in this book is film as a counter-argument to prevailing culture and norms. Film is a tool for re-imagining how we conceive of ourselves and the world around us. Even more, this book is about film at the centre of a social life of ideas. Through the lives of people in this book, we see how ideas emerge, who was responsible and how they have changed our thinking about film and media. The book is likewise about why theory and critical thinking matters, not just to film academics but to all of us working across the humanities. Most, if not all, of these people had a commitment to working with theory and applying theory to something concrete: initially film, but often in tandem with other counter movements such as feminism and avant-garde art. But why theory? Theory allowed for a rigorous analysis of modes of representation and showed us how the film and media affect us and bind us into particular ideas and attitudes. But this work didn't simply stop with theory and analysis. There was a focus on changing things through the application of theory to film. Looking back on it now, the work undertaken in and around the education department reads like a startlingly progressive enterprise which captured different fields and disciplines with education and teaching at the heart of the work. The extent to which this focused upon representation is indicative of the impact this work has had on culture and society in the twenty-first century.

As we will see, film was considered a primarily artisan craft in the early years of the BFI and much of the institution's early education initiatives were conducted with handiwork societies and adult education initiatives. This provided a rigorous scaffold for film to develop within the instruction, but it wasn't until the late 1950s when film started to annex theories and ideas from other disciplines and movements in order to legitimise it as an academic subject. From here on, I argue, the work of the Education Department is indicative of a distinct period in contemporary British history where ideas from abroad were welcomed at institutional level. It was a time when financial resources were made available to people working within the arts and humanities and they embarked upon work, theoretical and practical, which transformed the way we think about culture today. That the story is about the BFI is perhaps unsurprising: in the mid-twentieth century, film was a new art form, but it was largely ignored at academic level. Film was productively undisciplined, and it attracted many sharp minds, many of whom were taken in by the BFI's education department, which became a site for the exchange of ideas and concepts across a remarkable range of existing disciplines. Some of these names, such as Laura Mulvey, are well-known, but if this book is both indebted and sympathetic to one figure, it is Paddy Whannel who was the pioneering head of the education department from 1957 until his resignation in 1971. Whannel's work provided the scaffold for the innovation of film education both in Britain and the United States, yet he is a rather neglected figure. This book hopes to rectify this oversight.

Still, this book is more than a biographical sketch. *Film, In Theory* examines the BFI Education Department as a pivotal initiative in the formation of film studies. It is the study of the emergence of new intellectual paradigms – and the institutional resistance to them. It shows how efforts to develop a body of film research and writing informed by transnational developments in communications theory, Marxism, anthropology and semiotics were encouraged as a response to the apparent paucity of Anglophone endeavours in these fields. It constitutes a conscientious account of intellectual innovation and convergences at a deeply significant moment in the modernisation of British culture. It makes an account for the role of the BFI Education Department, and its sister organisation the Society for Education in Film and Television, as a crucial bridge between the established work of the New Left and the emergence of a film culture informed by continental theory.[2] It positions the work of the BFI Education Department as a quasi-academic space that used lecturing, research, administration, and an embrace of ideas and concepts as intellectual and cultural interventions. For the educators, writers and intellectuals at the very heart of this book, rigorous engagement with film was both the source of joy and satisfaction, but it also formed a problem: How can we develop and share this knowledge in a robust manner? This problematic was central to the Education Department's role throughout the late twentieth century as it engaged with vanguard approaches to film production and consumption, knowledge production and dissemination, and media and communications awareness. The BFI Education Department's staff members, along with those associated with SEFT, took on ambitious roles as the front persons for these innovative pursuits, and so much of their work, spanning disciplines and outputs, reckons with contentious ideas and concepts across the span of multimedia communication which continue to inform our ways of being and communicating in the twenty-first century.

This book periodises this era of innovation at the BFI Education Department from 1957, when Whannel was appointed, until 1989, when SEFT was shut down, with its outstanding responsibilities moved to the John Logie Baird Centre at the University of Glasgow, and a National Curriculum for England, Wales and Northern Ireland was implemented for primary, and later secondary,

2 The Society for Education in Film and Television hereafter referred to as SEFT.

schools. While much important work was undertaken by the department after 1989, this feels like the subject for another study. Furthermore, the era captured by this book exemplifies a form of institutional activity informed by and responding to post-war educational reform. The combination of the Butler Act of 1944 and the Newsom and Robbins Reports of 1963 provided a radical overhaul of education in Britain and opened up university places for those who would have been previously denied such opportunities. In the process, debates about the collision of popular culture and high art were shadowed by the endeavours to open up new theoretical and political spaces on the left after the crises of 1956 when the brutal crushing of the Hungarian Revolution shattered commitments to the Communist Party. The emergence of journals on the left in Britain allowed young intellectuals to think and write their way through these traumas. This led to institutions such as the BFI taking on board much of the ideas and energy, through employing individuals responsible for this movement, and allowing them the space to work and develop their ideas within a relatively secure setting. As we will see, this energy was not just directed towards the page or the screen. Coffee house culture, summer schools of film and even pubs in Soho were key areas of discourse and education, in providing social spaces for film culture to emerge and shape the BFI Education Department. It is within these social networks where we witness the broad perspectives of the key personnel so crucial to the institution's continued development and momentum and I have tried to preserve as much of this energy as possible through the interviews in this book.

It is curious, however, that so few institutional histories of the BFI, let alone its Education Department or *Screen* journal, exist. There are just two full-length critical studies: Ivan Butler's *To Encourage the Art of Film: The Story of the British Film Institute* (1971) is a sketchy history of the institution's formations and successes devoid of in-depth analysis, preferring a surface-level appreciation of the institution's achievements up to that point.[3] More recently, Christophe Dupin and Geoffrey Nowell-Smith's edited collection *The British Film Institute, the Government and Film Culture, 1933–2000* (2012) provides a far more detailed account often forensically so, of the institution's history through a series of essays on differing aspects of the institution's

[3] Ivan Butler, *To Encourage the Art of Film: The Story of the British Film Institute* (London: Hale, 1971).

history.[4] Dupin and Nowell-Smith's work is rigorous and lively but suffers from an inconsistency of tone – many of the chapters have different authors which makes it an uneven read. The book does feature the education department in a chapter written by Terry Bolas which is an extension on Bolas's earlier, monumental survey *Screen Education: From Film Appreciation to Media Studies* (2009).[5] Despite the richness of its institutional detail, both of Bolas's histories are hostile towards theoretical developments in the department and remain entangled in disputes from the time.[6]

My approach to this history was markedly different from the above accounts. I was not able to access the Education Department papers held within the BFI Archive, as they are now part of the Corporate Archive and therefore not available for consultation. This unexpected difficulty pivoted my focus away from the historical materials collected within the archive and towards the very much living and active figures who were so willing to give me their time to speak about the effects the BFI Education Department and *Screen* had on their intellectual, cultural and personal lives. Throughout 2023, I interviewed a broad range of people associated either directly, or indirectly, with the BFI Education Department during the period covered by this

[4] Geoffrey Nowell-Smith and Christophe Dupin (eds), *The British Film Institute, the Government and Film Culture, 1933–2000* (Manchester: Manchester University Press, 2012). Nowell-Smith is an important figure for this story and worked across the BFI in many roles from the 1960s through the 2000s.

[5] Terry Bolas, *Screen Education: From Film Appreciation to Media Studies* (Bristol: Intellect, 2009). Bolas was a secretary at SEFT in the late 1960s and was co-editor of *Screen* journal for a brief period in 1969.

[6] It is also important to note D. N. Rodowick's *The Crisis of Political Modernism; Criticism and Ideology in Contemporary Film Theory* (Berkeley: University of California Press, 1994). Rodowick, taking his cue from the film theorist Sylvia Harvey, defines 'political modernism' as the combination of 'semiotic and ideological analysis with the development of an avant-garde aesthetic practice dedicated to the production of radical social effects'. While Rodowick's discourse refers to neither a style nor a theory but a logic common to film theorists and film-makers since 1968, his account is indicative of a failure in intellectual histories of the era to accommodate the cycle of transposition, dissemination and eventual circulation of theory, particularly in Britain. Further, Rodowick does not account for the role of the institution in legitimising these processes of travelling theories through the range of cultural work being undertaken. While Rodowick insists that the emergence of theory can be traced to debates in French film theory occurring after the student revolts of 1968 which set in motion the programmatic shift of focus resulting in the emergence of *Screen* journal as an offshoot from the BFI Education Department in 1970, this book suggests an alternative history, less deferential to the international events of 1968 and one which is unique to Britain. See also Sylvia Harvey, 'Whose Brecht? Memories for the Eighties', *Screen* 23, no. 1 (May–June 1981): pp. 45–59.

book.[7] The processes of listening and attention which underpin these conversations provide the engine for what follows.

But I do not intend this book to be a sad-eyed love letter to theory, or even to a supposed heyday of the 1970s. *Film, In Theory* illustrates how ideas are attached to individuals who can form a collective and work within an institution in the form of a rupture, displacing an orthodoxy and replacing it with something entirely new. For the BFI Education Department and *Screen*, it was an overhaul of benign forms of criticism often summarised as film appreciation (although this history offered by some interviewees suggests that this term was as much part of the transformation of film culture as it was an antidote). It also shows how the hugely important journals *Screen* and *Screen Education*, which were published by SEFT and published Laura Mulvey's 'Visual Culture and Narrative Pleasure' essay in autumn 1975, formed a homogenising effect of unifying concepts and ideas and political concerns within the pages of a journal, allowing it to be a force which orients so many differing areas of cultural and intellectual work. In drawing on interviews so extensively, and analyses of archival material where possible, the book allows us to analyse this work through the exceptionally strong memories and recollections of those involved who are still in a position to share their accounts with us. It shows us how the sociological antagonism generated by new and unorthodox intellectual and social paradigms has a recent history in Britain and sets these innovations and conflicts within their wider historical context. My aim is also to convey some of the sheer joy of encountering exciting and compelling new theories and concepts from abroad, working collectively and contentiously to figure it all out, and showcasing how an engagement with difficult ideas does not have to be an austere and sobering experience. Hopefully, some of the real energy from this era comes across in the book.

And this energy, described by more than one person I spoke to as 'intoxicating' had very specific effects. It provided the space and rationale for legitimising film in the academy and school systems; for mobilising feminist counter cinemas; for the writing and dissemination of pamphlets, directories,

[7] Indeed, the methodology of this book would be considered invalid especially if one adheres to the positions taken by *Screen* in the mid-1970s. Empiricism was not considered a legitimate form of analysis as were the anecdotal and the idea of common sense. This book is indebted to the anecdotal in its methodology.

articles and books on topics such as the Western, queer cinema, Black cinema, genre and iconography; for the physical constructing film extracts for teachers to use in the classroom and travelling the length of Britain providing extra-mural courses in film; and for an entire transformation of the ways in which we think about film and the world.

# 1

# The formation of the BFI

During the interwar period, film emerged as a popular, industrial, technological medium of artistic expression throughout Europe. The role of the film-maker was viewed as parallel to that of an artisan or engineer.[1] It is within these conditions that the British Film Institute was founded in 1933. Indeed, the very existence of the BFI has its roots in the adult education world as it was founded as an adjunct of both the Association of Scientific Workers and the British Institute of Adult Education. They, along with around one hundred local organisations involved in science and education, were conscious of the impending effects of the introduction of sound technology on filmgoers across the country and set up a Commission on Education and Cultural Films in 1929. The commission set to work, organising conferences, developing links with government departments and technical workers, and receiving funding from sources including the Trustees of the Carnegie United Kingdom Trust, public education authorities and a handful of voluntary organisations. A report was published in 1932 entitled 'The Film In National Life' which had a firm recommendation: an institution of film ought to be established to promote various uses of the film as a 'contribution to national well-being', to provide a permanent independent body for educational and cultural purposes and to consider 'methods for raising the standard of public appreciation of films'.[2]

This was a rich period for the development of film at an institutional level across Europe. National institutes of film were founded not just in London but also in Berlin, Moscow and Paris, with these structures more

[1] Perhaps prefiguring the more priestly auteur conception of the film director which emerged in the late 1950s.

[2] Commission on Educational and Cultural Films, *The Film in National Life* (London: George Allen & Unwin, 1932). See also Nowell-Smith and Dupin, *The British Film Institute, the Government, and Film Culture*, p. 15.

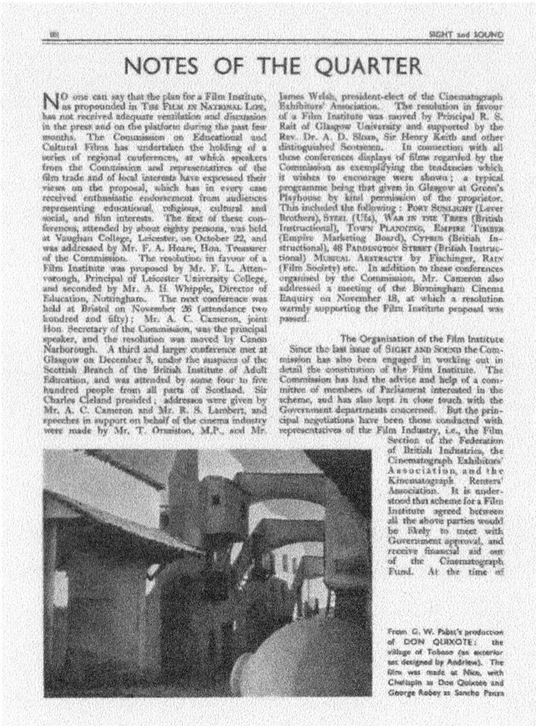

SIGHT and SOUND

NOTES OF THE QUARTER

NO one can say that the plan for a Film Institute, as propounded in THE FILM IN NATIONAL LIFE, has not received adequate ventilation and discussion in the press and on the platform during the past few months. The Commission on Educational and Cultural Films has undertaken the holding of a series of regional conferences, at which speakers from the Commission and representatives of the film trade and of local interests have expressed their views on the proposal, which has in every case received enthusiastic endorsement from audiences representing educational, religious, cultural and social, and film interests. The first of these conferences, attended by about eighty persons, was held at Vaughan College, Leicester, on October 22, and was addressed by Mr. F. A. Hoare, Hon. Treasurer of the Commission. The resolution in favour of a Film Institute was proposed by Mr. F. L. Attenborough, Principal of Leicester University College, and seconded by Mr. A. H. Whipple, Director of Education, Nottingham. The next conference was held at Bristol on November 26 (attendance two hundred and fifty); Mr. A. C. Cameron, joint Hon. Secretary of the Commission, was the principal speaker, and the resolution was moved by Canon Narborough. A third and larger conference met at Glasgow on December 3, under the auspices of the Scottish Branch of the British Institute of Adult Education, and was attended by some four to five hundred people from all parts of Scotland. Sir Charles Cleland presided; addresses were given by Mr. A. C. Cameron and Mr. R. S. Lambert, and speeches in support on behalf of the cinema industry were made by Mr. T. Ormiston, M.P., and Mr. James Welsh, president-elect of the Cinematograph Exhibitors' Association. The resolution in favour of a Film Institute was moved by Principal R. S. Rait of Glasgow University and supported by the Rev. Dr. A. D. Sloan, Sir Henry Keith and other distinguished Scotsmen. In connection with all these conferences displays of films regarded by the Commission as exemplifying the tendencies which it wishes to encourage were shown; a typical programme being that given in Glasgow at Green's Playhouse by kind permission of the proprietor. This included the following: PORT SUNLIGHT (Lever Brothers), STEEL (Ufa), WAR IN THE TREES (British Instructional), TOWN PLANNING, EMPIRE TIMBER (Empire Marketing Board), CYPRUS (British Instructional), 48 PADDINGTON STREET (British Instructional) MUSICAL ABSTRACTS by Fischinger, RAIN (Film Society) etc. In addition to these conferences organised by the Commission, Mr. Cameron also addressed a meeting of the Birmingham Cinema Enquiry on November 18, at which a resolution warmly supporting the Film Institute proposal was passed.

The Organisation of the Film Institute

Since the last issue of SIGHT AND SOUND the Commission has also been engaged in working out in detail the constitution of the Film Institute. The Commission has had the advice and help of a committee of members of Parliament interested in the scheme, and has also kept in close touch with the Government departments concerned. But the principal negotiations have been those conducted with representatives of the Film Industry, i.e., the Film Section of the Federation of British Industries, the Cinematograph Exhibitors' Association, and the Kinematograph Renters' Association. It is understood that scheme for a Film Institute agreed between all the above parties would be likely to meet with Government approval, and receive financial aid out of the Cinematograph Fund. At the time of

From G. W. Pabst's production of DON QUIXOTE: the village of Toboso (an exterior set designed by Andrieu). The film was made at Nice, with Chaliapin as Don Quixote and George Robey as Sancho Panza

**Figure 1** Announcement of the new British Film Institute, *Sight and Sound*, Winter 1933.

often than not incorporating national film archives and film libraries. These institutions were similar in articulating strident concepts of nation, film and education citizenship, and, according to film historian Haidee Wasson, 'formalised the earliest discussion of cinema's role in modern institutions of state, crystalizing on-going debates which co-articulated film with ideals of nation, history, collection, and education'.[3] Education was a connective bridge in this correspondence between the nation and film; the Italian government also proposed establishing an International Educational Cinematographic Institute as an instrument of the League of Nations which was heavily invested in by both the British and Italian governments. This institute's journal, the *International Review of Educational Cinematography*, heavily promoted uses of film for educational purposes, providing information around the

[3] Haidee Wasson, *Museum Movies: The Museum of Modern Art and the Birth of Art Cinema* (Berkeley: University of California Press, 2005), p. 7.

lack of available teacher training for those wishing to use visual aids while also providing space for advertising adult education courses on 'Cinema Culture'; indeed, a 1932 issue of the journal contained a proposal by Sir James Marchant and Sir Oswald Stoll for a People's Cinema University in London. This concept suggested a remarkable institute for film consisting of a central building equipped with lecture halls where 'sound-film installations … would radiate'; a central dome with a Zeiss planetarium; and a suite of reading rooms and offices which would house film societies. The institute would be designed by Sir Giles Gilbert Scott, responsible for hugely significant work on the New Bodleian Library, Battersea Power Station, Liverpool Cathedral and designed perhaps the most iconic of British symbols: the red telephone box. Education was at the centre of the idea which promised to create 'an expert educational board to meet the requirements of teachers and scholars and would be distributed and collected by motor cinema vans throughout the country'. Projectors would also be supplied to schools, churches, and institutions. 'Sir James believes,' the advertisement concluded, 'that the time is ripe for a People's Cinema University which, in its own sphere, would attempt work resembling that of the BBC.'[4]

Despite Marchant's wonderfully ambitious concept, of which little other evidence appears to exist, the actual birth of an Institute for Film in Britain was realised in altogether more reduced circumstances: on the first floor of a rented premises at 4 Great Russell Street in central London in October 1933. The institute was formed with ten official objectives:

1. To act as a clearing house for information on all matters affecting films at home and abroad, particularly as regards education and general culture
2. To influence public opinion to appreciate the value of films as entertainment and instruction
3. To advise educational institutions and other organisations and persons on films and apparatus
4. To link up the film trade and the cultural and educational interests of the country

[4] For more on this fanciful idea, see James Marchant, *The Cinema in Education: Being the Report of the Psychological Investigation Conducted by Special Subcommittees Appointed by the Cinema Commission of Enquiry Established by the National Council of Public Morals* (London: Allen & Unwin, 1925).

118 SIGHT and SOUND

In the offices of the British Film Institute, 4, Great Russell Street, London

the Carnegie U. K. Trustees and several national educational bodies, as well as to loans from two principal cinema trade organisations. This help was generously given to enable the Institute to get upon its feet. Now that it has done so it has applied for the further sums which it requires now for the performance of its duties to that source which Parliament provided in 1932, in expectation of the Institute's coming into being. The British Film Institute has applied for a grant from the Cinematograph Fund set up under the Sunday Performances Act.

This Fund, we may remind our readers, was constituted to be used by the Privy Council "to promote the development of the film as a means of entertainment and instruction." Only one body exists in this country for the express purpose of translating these words into effect: and this body is the Film Institute, in whose Articles of Association (as approved by the Board of Trade) the above phrase is specifically quoted as describing its main function. Nor should it be forgotten that the twelve months preceding the registration of the Institute were taken up not merely with negotiations between the film industry and the educational interests concerned, but also with frequent informal recourse for advice and guidance to members of H.M. Government and to Government Departments, in order that the new Institute might come into being, not indeed under direct State control, but at least with the implied approval and sanction of the State—and therefore under its responsibility.

The British Film Institute then is, by its history and by its constitution, directly linked to the Cinematograph Fund—a link which formed the principal, if not the only theme discussed during the debates in both Houses of Parliament on the establishment of the Fund. We may be pardoned for calling attention to these facts, but there will be other claims upon the Fund, some of them arising from private commercial sources, and others from disinterested sources. In regard to the latter, we suggest that, if there are any special pieces of work which the Privy Council wishes to encourage apart from the programme of the Film Institute, it would be logical to earmark funds for this work as a part of the main grant to the Film Institute, charging the latter with responsibility for reporting and advising upon the subsequent execution of this work, and for ensuring proper co-ordination with its own activities.

**Figure 2** The offices of the new British Film Institute, *Sight and Sound*, Winter 1934.

5. To encourage research into the various uses of the film
6. To establish a national repository of films of permanent value
7. To provide a descriptive and critical catalogue of films of educational and cultural value
8. To advise government departments concerned with films
9. To certify films as educational, cultural or scientific
10. To undertake similar duties in relation to the Empire

The objectives of the new institute indicate just how central the concept of national well-being was to its activities. It was also quite clearly tied up with education and this was to be the emphasis across the BFI's early years at Great Russell Street. A sub-committee was formed to explore the possibility of a children's film company, and talks were held concerning the development of a course in cinematography at the University of London. The previous year, the British Institute of Adult Education had founded a publication called *Sight and Sound* as a quarterly review of modern aids to learning, but the nascent BFI took over the publication of the journal from 1934, re-casting it as a magazine solely devoted to film.

The BFI's formation was a form of institutionalising mission which allowed for an appropriation of film by an entire nation and an affirmation of national identity through the moving image. The BFI was founded upon this presupposition that film had a fundamentally pedagogical role to play in the formation of a robust national character, and without any competition, the institution was able to assume a cultural authority in the presentation, preservation and education of film on a national level in Britain.[5] As film was a developing art form, the film institute had no specific antecedents, yet the case for its creation rested 'on the belief that constructive action to encourage films is better than restrictive action to discourage bad ones'. How did the institute define these terms? The role of pedagogy within the BFI emerged in a parallel fashion to the documentary movement of the 1930s and continued to be expressed more explicitly through publications such as Roger Manvell's *Film* (1944) and *The Film and the Public* (1955) and Ernest Lindgren's *Art of the Film* (1948). The underpinning assumption of Manvell and Lindgren's work was that films played a crucial role in 'the formation of false social and moral values by children and young people' and the film educator ought to operate in a censorious role, and lead children towards 'good films' and away from 'bad films'.[6] Accordingly, the role of those working in film education was to provide a filter between the messages of these films and their consumption by the youth, inculcating an ability to discriminate between the 'good' and the 'bad'. This ability was centred upon the term 'film appreciation' which was the BFI's preferred method of cultural consumption. Film appreciation was a largely elusive concept. Appreciation as a means of enjoying and understanding art

[5] By this, I mean there was no other national institution of film operating within Britain at that time. However, there was a very lively culture of film societies operating throughout the country. See Richard Lowell MacDonald, *The Appreciation of Film: The Postwar Film Society Movement and Film Culture in Britain* (Exeter: University of Exeter Press, 2016).

[6] Roger Manvell, *Film* (London: Pelican, 1944); Manvell, *The Film and the Public* (London: Pelican, 1955); Ernest Lindgren, *Art of the Film* (London: Allen and Unwin, 1948). Lindgren was the first curator of the National Film Archive and remained in this role until his death in 1973. *The Wheare Report*, published in 1950 to confront censorship, further imposed this moralistic view of film, stating that 'a large number of films are exposing children regularly to the suggestion that the highest values in life are riches, power, luxury and public adulation … this general kind of easy and selfish philosophy is fringed with other supporting illusions involving the distortion of history and biography and of people of other nations and their national heroes'.

had been in use since the late nineteenth century and gained a popularity through commercially successful essay collections such as the art critic Walter Pater's *Appreciations, with an Essay on Style.*[7] To this day, the term indicates a level of connoisseurship, a shorthand for the detached criticisms of the leisure classes or, more damagingly, a front for disinterested generalisations, a series of close readings devoid of context. Richard MacDonald speculates how film appreciation existed in an 'ambiguous zone' between the possession of discrimination and sensitivity and the process of study, acquiring knowledge and understanding, involving the acceptance of a pre-defined canon.[8] Appreciation was, by its very nature, somewhat ill-defined, yet the term does considerable heavy lifting throughout the British Film Institute's inaugural decades; as we will see, it was to become a term to be chaffed against as the Education Department searched for more sophisticated methods of analysis in the 1960s.[9]

But it would be reductive to simply dismiss the work of the BFI in its early years as merely naive. From the beginning, the Education Department worked where the National Film Archive, which was founded in 1935 by Ernest Lindgren, ended in disseminating film, and film stills, to schools and adult education centres around Britain – one which was especially necessary outside of London. The department allowed documentaries, instructive films on art and science, amateur films, and television recordings to be used by students, independent researchers or those working in the industry and worked in tandem with the flourishing film society movements across the country. This work was undertaken as a proxy for the complete lack of film education in schools and at third level.

Of course, the BFI was also founded at a time when the British documentary film, specifically the pioneering work of the Scottish director John Grierson, who had coined the term 'documentary', was hugely influential on the development of a form of film production steeped in the 'realism' of the everyday. During

7 Walter Pater, *Appreciations, with an Essay on Style* (London: Macmillan, 1889).

8 MacDonald, *The Appreciation of Film*, p. 15. In this instance the canon would have been the lending catalogue of the National Film Library.

9 Film appreciation at the BFI would later be more memorably termed as the 'we-know-whats-good-and-don't-need-to-spell-it-out attitude'. See 'Two Steps Forward, One Step Back: Cultural Struggle in the BFI', *Journal of Popular British Cinema* 4, ed. James Chapman and Christine Geraghty (2001): pp. 112–27.

the same year as the BFI's foundation, Grierson brought his documentary unit to the General Post Office which had major implications for its output, as it allowed for the setting up of sponsored documentaries primarily related to postal work and inspired the creation of other documentary units which were branded together as the Crown Film Unit in 1939. These units played a vital role in communication information during the war and the importance of documentary to British cinema was highlighted in a *Times* editorial which asserted that the 'film of fact … was the distinctively British contribution to the art of the moving pictures. English producers of fiction films can scarcely do more than show America that they have mastered a technique that was first developed in Hollywood; those who make films of fact, on the other hand, go to New York to teach … British producers are acknowledged to hold the hegemony in this branch of their work.'[10]

These documentary films had a distinct function: illustrating a reality of social life or the director's personal vision with a robust sense of ethics and morals. As the *Times* editorial indicates, this work was seen as a rebuttal to Hollywood which, in this context, represented the very worst excesses of film. The technical expertise and craftsmanship of American films was trivial in the face of the direct, educative work of British documentary film. The broadcasting of a strong, singular message, steeped in integrity and real social issues was the underpinning of this conception of cinema. This approach was central to the BFI's education policy throughout the interwar and immediate post-war era where there were two positions which influenced the work of film educators at the BFI which we will refer to as the Leavis position and the Film Language position.

## F. R. Leavis and Film Language

The Leavis position was overwhelmingly influential in British culture in the first half of the twentieth century. It was founded upon Matthew Arnold's ideas in *Culture and Anarchy* and developed by F. R. Leavis and his associates in the

10 Quoted in Charles Barr, *A Very Short Introduction to British Cinema* (Oxford: Oxford University Press, 2023), p. 37.

1930s.[11] Leavis's position insisted that modern society is profoundly unstable because its industrial nature disallows it from meeting important human needs. We are separated from one another, from our work, and from nature, an opposition expressed in the opposition between mechanics and organics. But it is only art – which, for Leavis, was properly realised through the work of D. H. Lawrence – which allows us to critique this situation. This form of criticism is important as it provides space for the artist to articulate their position while also allowing the critic to develop their own sensibilities. Underpinning this belief is the idea that great art is an expression of great moral values. Therefore, the critic's task is both artistic and moral and no real separation exists between the two. The person who is making such rich and fine distinctions about art will be able equally to make similar distinctions in life.

Leavis makes literary criticism the moral centre of education and assumes the most profound critics of society will emerge from scholars in this field even if it is aligned with other fields such as the visual arts. His position is hierarchical; he is essentially looking down on any artistic expression which, under his terms, is not high art. This division is most explicitly stated in *Culture and Environment* which is strikingly critical of 'new' forms of expression, particularly advertising and journalism. These professions are accused of exhibiting false moral values through the use of corrupting language. Here lies the inverse of Leavis's moral standpoint: corrupting language automatically means bad morals. In his terms, if language is used correctly through artistic expression, one can make fine moral distinctions. Leavis's position was taken up so comprehensively because it is coherent and allows for direct pedagogical interventions: primarily protecting children from corrupting influences through the development of critical thinking and allowing them to develop their full potential.

As we will see, this application of this method to film education would provide theoretical issues for film educators at the BFI. But it also provided a position to work against. Leavis's position was largely hostile to technology and

[11] Matthew Arnold, *Culture and Anarchy* (Oxford: Oxford University Press, 2006). F. R. Leavis and Denys Thompson's *Culture and Environment* (London: Chatto & Windus, 1962), along with Leavis's own pamphlet *Mass Civilisation and Minority Culture* (Cambridge: Minority Press, 1930) and book *Education and the University: A Sketch for an 'English School* (London: Chatto & Windus, 1948) were also indicative of this position.

mass media and it sees art as the direct personal expression of an individual and the influence of any form of media – film, television – cannot be taken as 'art'. Secondly, what were Leavis's own moral values? Were they permanently etched ideals or were they concepts and ideas rooted in the 1930s? For Leavis, the ideal 'man' was traditional and able to make fine moral discriminations which work in favour of a general moral and cultural health. Film education, therefore, becomes an attempt to encourage people to adopt a certain set of values. Yet these values are implicit, they are not visible for inspection, they are merely assumed and not argued. Furthermore, the values are the property of a cultured, puritan, middle-class English worldview. Because these values are the scaffold for a form of critical judgement, they demonstrate a preference for certain types of art. Leavis certainly favours the restraint and discipline of Jane Austen over the uncertainties of Emily Bronte; transposed to film, this legitimises the emphasis towards documentary and social realism as opposed to fantasy, Westerns, science fiction, thrillers and Hollywood films. The aesthetic without the moral, for Leavis, becomes immoral. The Leavisian method eschews any form of critical apparatus, yet it is easy to mimic – much of this involves simply quoting a passage and speculating about the author's intentions.

Meanwhile, the Film Language approach derived its methods from the social documentary movement of the 1930s which, in turn, took its ideas from Sergei Eisenstein's writings about the cinema in the Soviet Union. But the British interpretation of Eisenstein's work, at this juncture, was firmly rooted in an industrial analysis of the technical side of film: shots, cuts, fades, dissolves and limited discussions of the role played by each member of the crew: director, set designer, sound-recordist. This approach was direct, necessary – especially for young learners – for the time but devoid of sophistication. However, the Film Language does offer a history of cinema, through its technical developments – an alternative tradition is constructed from D. W. Griffith through Soviet cinema and German expressionist cinema of the 1920s and later through the work of Orson Welles. Yet this only allows for a limited, naive analysis of thematic concerns as the method offers no way of interpreting the themes.

Film education at the BFI was essentially a form of righteous education. The institution's work could not shake the burden of morality. As we will see, Leavis later became a dirty word in the department, but it is foolish to ignore the positive impacts of this approach. The Leavis intellectual world, particularly up to the mid- to the late 1950s, was instrumental in providing a rationale for workers both within and adjunct to the Education Department to form a lecturing agency and simply go out to cities and towns across the country, teaching interested people about film. It was through this commitment to Leavis which drew together people such as Stuart Hall, a committed Leavisite on leaving Oxford in the late 1950s, together with Paddy Whannel and Alan Lovell, a peace activist, film critic and housemate of Hall at Oxford. Lovell was to work across a myriad of roles within BFI Education and *Screen*. When I spoke with Alan Lovell in early 2020, he vividly recalled this era of the BFI. 'When I knew Stuart closely,' he said, 'we were very much part of the Leavisite intellectual world. We were proud Leavisites, left-Leavisites. But under the influence of Richard Hoggart and Raymond Williams we [started] to move away from Leavis and have a more positive attitude to working-class culture and mass culture generally.'

Here, Lovell points to an important shift. The dual publication of Richard Hoggart's *The Uses of Literacy* and Raymond Williams's *Culture and Society* between 1957 and 1958 was hugely transformative for intellectuals on the left.[12] Both books promoted an idea of 'culture' as a way of life, as a community's way of expressing itself. Hoggart and Williams drew on their own childhood experiences, in Leeds and Abergavenny, respectively, and on their engagement with Leavisite ideals, expressing that culture is both ordinary and a way of life and allows meaning to take shape to their social existence. Hoggart, in particular, wrote eloquently about his attachment to the working-class culture which defined his own upbringing and the form of shock, or even whiplash, he experienced when, after the Butler Education Act of 1944, he was granted access to more privileged forms of education; Williams, on the other hand, used a form of historical analysis to inquire how the meaning of culture was a vital and consistent wheel in British cultural and intellectual history. Both writers concluded with a desire for a return to a more organic form of living

[12] Richard Hoggart, *The Uses of Literacy* (Harmondsworth: Penguin, 1958); Raymond Williams, *Culture and Society, 1780–1950* (Harmondsworth: Penguin, 1958).

culture – one which was hostile to the encroachment of mass media and American culture.[13]

The influence and impact of Hoggart and Williams on a generation of writers and educators, especially Paddy Whannel, was immense. But prior to Whannel's arrival, a shift in policy at the BFI had also occurred through the appointment of Stanley Reed as the first head of the Education Department in 1950. Reed was keen to encourage the development of film study at every level of education and introduced a policy of publishing pamphlets on methods of film education, one which was to continue throughout the following decades. He also prepared the groundwork for schools to teach film through the preparation of extracts from feature films. Reed played a crucial role in forming the Society of Film Teachers – soon to become the Society for Education in Film and Television or SEFT – which further emboldened the study of film in schools. The Society of Film Teachers was founded following a one-day conference organised by the English New Education Fellowship at the University of London's Institute of Education. Membership was available to all those who were actively engaged in education using film across schools, colleges and youth services. The BFI offered the organisation a modest grant and SFT was re-inaugurated as SEFT in 1958 in order to pursue matters concerning 'Screen education'.

For the most part, SEFT was run by a committee composed of primary and secondary school teachers, working in their own free time, and from their own homes. Despite the voluntary nature of the organisation, it was quickly productive in developing a range of materials to aid the use of film in education. The most significant of these journals was birthed in 1959, *Screen Education*, which runs to this day as *Screen*. Its first issue reflected a familiar moral tone in expressing a need for caution on the impact of screen media on the young and declaring the role of teachers to be that of interpreters, facilitating the development of children as 'intelligent viewers'. While initially a pamphlet, SEFT continued to produce *Screen Education* throughout the early 1960s, with the journal increasing in size and influence along the way. During this

[13] Hoggart was particularly despairing of American culture. His depictions of British youth lurking ominously in 'harshly-lit milk-bars', as they socialised through a 'peculiarly thin and pallid form of dissipation', on their way to a complete 'aesthetic breakdown' reminds me of Don DeLillo's bleak sci-fi novels decamped to post-war Britain. See *The Uses of Literacy*, pp. 247–8.

time, SEFT produced other informative journals such as *Film & TV News* and handbooks on film production and film societies. But from the mid-1960s, it was decreed by the BFI that SEFT should be allowed to have its own full-time paid secretary and a registered office in London, under the umbrella of the BFI. This proved to be a significant development for film education in Britain as it effectively annexed SEFT as part of the BFI Education Department, which would prove to be a fruitful, if often uneasy alliance in the decades to come.

## The New Left and film education

The combination of a Leavisite approach to film education along with the paucity of options for those wishing to pursue the study of film in Britain was a moot topic for the BFI Education Department.[14] But it was the appointment of Paddy Whannel to the Education Department in 1957 which was the single most important event for the development of film as a serious site for study and critical analysis in Britain. Born into a working-class family in Pitlochry, Perthshire, 70 miles north of Edinburgh, Whannel finished his official schooling in 1937 at the age of fourteen and immediately commenced work as a film projectionist at the Royal Theatre in his hometown. His wartime national service was as part of the British Royal Navy and he subsequently qualified as a teacher in 1948 whereupon he moved to London, securing a diploma in art history at the University of London in 1948. He also commenced teaching work at a number of London secondary schools, teaching media, film and social studies. On his appointment to the BFI in 1957, he was appointed to

[14] In a pamphlet published by the department in 1964, entitled *Film Teaching*, Paddy Whannel succinctly summed up this problem:

> Concepts of film language and of theories of montage, ideal for describing the techniques of Soviet silent cinema, are now seen as inadequate when confronted by a film maker like Renoir … there is still a tendency, that is, when talking about the cinema to separate the method of presentation from the intrinsic quality of what is being said. What we are striving for now in film education is a way of talking about the cinema as a whole experience, of discussing style not as something imposed upon as subject already given but as the way in which a director conveys to us his inner meanings … The kind of film teaching we are dealing with here is to be seen as part of a general cultural education. It is not designed as a professional or specialist education. This country still makes no provision for training film makers: there is still no national film school. Yet experience tells us there is a connection between the films a country produces and the idea of cinema in the public mind.

its Film Appreciation and Distribution Department. On his resignation in 1971, he relinquished the post of head of the Education Department. Within these fourteen years, Whannel's rare skills as educationist, administrator, critic and – perhaps more crucially – *animateur*, allowed the BFI to flourish as a quasi-academic space, providing a fertile terrain for intellectuals working with film to comprehensively rethink our understanding of the form. Laura Mulvey, who worked closely with Whannel during the 1960s, says:

> One of the things that has always interested me about Paddy is that he was extremely influential but never actually wrote [much]. These people get forgotten. I am always interested in these people who become more shadow figures as time goes on. They never really committed themselves to writing. You can be a really influential intellectual but if you don't write anything no one remembers you. Paddy was like that. He had a really key influence on that generation of young, up and coming film critics and theorists. He had an extraordinary instinct for what they could do. He could always understand how things could be brought together.[15]

The scope of Whannel's interests in and experience with popular culture enabled him to forge an alliance with the formative New Left. Through his writings for the nascent *New Left Review*, Whannel was part of a cohort linked to the *Universities and Left Review* journal, centring their focus around class politics and activism, socialising at the Partisan Coffee House in Soho. This journal, along with the *New Reasoner*, had been formed in an attempt to create an intellectual alternative on the left, after the shock of Khruschev's secret speech in February 1956, which had revealed Stalin's Great Purges, among other acts of terror, and the brutal crushing of the Hungarian uprising later that year. Laura Mulvey recalls the first meeting of the *Universities and Left Review* taking place simultaneously to Bill Haley's first tour of the UK – a tantalising crossover of cultural events, even if, on further research, the dates do not appear to entirely match up.[16] But the increasing appeal of American culture, through the circulation of Hollywood cinema and rock n' roll, was heralded by the spectacular success of singer Haley's *Rock Around the Clock* film which played to delirious audiences in the UK throughout the autumn of

[15] Laura Mulvey, personal interview, 6 November 2023.
[16] Ibid.

**FORUM 4: THE VISUAL PERSUADERS.** National Film Theatre, May 3rd—10th, 1959.
An 8-day Forum on **CINEMA** and **TELEVISION** as **ART** and **COMMUNICATION** is being presented at the invitation of the British Film Institute by the **Joint Council for Education Through Art.** The programme will include films, film extracts, Television transmissions, demonstrations, discussion and speakers engaged in Film, T.V., Criticism and Education.

The Forum will define the responsibilities of those who produce, assess and consume the products of cinema and television.

| | | | |
|---|---|---|---|
| *Sessions* | Sunday May 3rd | 11.00—5.30 p.m. | COMMUNITY AND COMMUNICATION |
| | Sunday May 3rd | 6.30 p.m. | HUMANISM—THE MAINSTREAM OF CINEMA |
| | Monday May 4th | 6.30 p.m. | CREATIVE WORKSHOP |
| | Tuesday May 5th | 6.00 p.m. | FACE IN THE MIRROR |
| | Wednesday May 6th | 6.00 p.m. | SCREEN TEST |
| | Thursday May 7th | 6.00 p.m. | BREAK THROUGH? (Can the new writers save the cinema?) |
| | Friday May 8th | 6.00 p.m. | POPULAR IMAGES |
| | Saturday May 9th | 10.30—1.00 p.m. | THE SWEET SMELL OF SUCCESS: TV and the Child. |
| | Saturday May 9th | 3.30 p.m. | TEENAGERS: PROBLEMS OR PEOPLE? |
| | Saturday May 9th | 7.30 p.m. | WAR ON THE SCREEN. A film analysed. |
| | Sunday May 10th | 10.30—1.00 p.m. | PRESSURE ON THE ARTIST |
| | Sunday May 10th | 2.30 p.m. | WHO CARES? |
| | Sunday May 10th | 6.30 p.m. | SOMETHING TO SING ABOUT? |

Speakers at the above sessions will include:

| | | | |
|---|---|---|---|
| Raymond Williams | Richard Roud | John Berger | Philip Purser |
| Karel Reisz | Leslie Mallory | Derek Hill | Tom Driberg |
| Stanley Reed | Brian Groombridge | John Huntley | Alan Lovell |
| Stuart Hall | | | |

For full details apply to the Education Officer, British Film Institute, 4, Great Russell Street, W.C.1. COVent Garden 2801.

**Figure 3** Outline for The Visual Persuaders conference, May 1959.

1956. The consistent popularity of cinema as a social pastime was concurrent with the exposure to American music beyond the novelty value of Bill Haley and his Comets – the likes of Chuck Berry and Little Richard also made their UK chart debuts in the late 1950s. This dual discovery of both Hollywood and American pop music was intoxicating for English teenagers born around the beginnings of the Second World War and who were coming of age in the later 1950s; this is reflected in not just the likes of the Rolling Stones appropriating American Black blues singers but also in the later allusions to Hollywood in British pop art through Richard Hamilton and Pauline Boty. Paddy Whannel was uniquely tuned into these forms of cultural crossovers, as well versed in contemporary jazz as contemporary film, even writing a series of articles for *Teaching* magazine in the early 1960s under the pseudonym Albert Casey – a reference to the jazz guitarist Al Casey.[17] But for the BFI, this indicated that their new head of department was singularly plugged into a whole range of cultural endeavours of which film was just one strand. Whannel's interests allowed the department to steer itself towards Hollywood, towards New Left

17 See Daniel Horowitz, 'From Workers and Literature to Youth and Popular Culture', in *Consuming Pleasures: Intellectuals and Popular Culture in the Postwar World* (Pennsylvania: University of Pennsylvania Press, 2012), pp. 235–70.

movements and maintain a conviction that the central terrain of socialist struggle was now on cultural and intellectual terms.

An emblematic moment for the BFI Education Department occurred in spring 1959. The Joint Council for Education through Art organised an eight-day conference called 'Visual Persuaders', held at the National Film Theatre in London. 'The aim of the forum, according to its organiser John Morley, was to develop a substantial body of public opinion that will share our vision of the role of arts in education and the part that this education plays in our mass society'.[18] Following the guidelines of the 1944 Education Act, Morley spoke at length about the crucial connections which need to be strengthened between education and art forms, suggesting that those working in schools need to become more attuned to the nuances of their students' upbringing and use this as a tool to develop more of an understanding of both film and television. Once the forum had concluded, the organisers released a statement announcing that 'the potential for research, study and enjoyment of film and television had been emphatically demonstrated'. Attendees of the forum were drawn from teachers and NFT members while speakers included Peter Worsley from the *New Reasoner* journal and Alan Lovell, Stuart Hall, Graham Martin, and John Berger, all of whom were contributors to *Universities and Left Review*. Members of the *Universities and Left Review* clubs were also present among the 5,500 attendees. The significant numbers attested to both the increasing interest in sophisticated analysis of culture and communications and the attendant needs for political mobilisation in the light of the events of 1956. But the conference also indicated a dissatisfaction with the BFI Education Department's methods. An editorial in *Screen Education* noted that 'several speakers at the forum bandied about the term "film appreciation' as if was a dirty expression', while also reflecting that there was 'more than a hint of passivity in "film appreciation", a feeling of it being mainly concerned with techniques and technicalities'.[19]

Raymond Williams, who also spoke at the conference, had already highlighted these concerns in an earlier article. Stating his experience in

18 Quoted in MacDonald, *The Appreciation of Film*, p. 173. Much of the information on this conference is detailed in MacDonald's account. For a first-hand account, see John Morley, 'Visual Persuaders', *Film* (September–October 1959): p. 6.

19 'Editorial', *Screen Education* 1 (1959): p. 2.

organising film appreciation classes for the Workers' Educational Association, Williams insisted that the 'small body of serious appreciatory work … [was] to one trained in literary criticism … likely to seem inadequate'. He continued: 'It is technically expert, but this advantage is limited by a common failure to understand the place of technical analysis in a total judgment – the film is interesting because of the emotional judgment with which it deals; it is also, technically, very competent.' Williams's reservations ran deep; he felt that 'appreciation' had generated a method of relating to the arts which was akin to 'deportment classes … what mattered was that the uninstructed (the lesser breeds who read the penny papers) should learn under the guidance of experts the finer points of an art which must be accepted as absolute'.

The Visual Persuaders conference reflects then-contemporary New Left concerns. It offered a space for a rethinking of culture as a keyword emerging from class, agency, experience and value. The conference itself was indicative of an increasing awareness on the New Left of cultural analysis, buoyed by the concurrent success of Hoggart's *The Uses of Literacy* and Williams's *Culture and Society*. Furthermore, the conference itself ensured that a serious engagement with popular culture beyond film appreciation was a tangible aim and this began to take shape within the Left-public intellectual sphere. But it was the publication of Hall and Whannel's *The Popular Arts* in 1964, which, in effect, was a packaging of the ideas formulated at the Visual Persuaders conference five years previously, which truly set the BFI Education Department on a path away from appreciation, even tentatively away from Leavis, and into far more capacious territory.

## The Popular Arts

Paddy Whannel and Stuart Hall collaborated throughout 1962 and 1963 on writing a book that would prove hugely influential for both the BFI Education Department and our conception of treating film as a serious topic for study. Formed from both their own interests in popular culture and their experiences in teaching film courses at adult education level across the country, *The Popular Arts*, published in 1964, is a pioneering study of popular culture and the first book to acknowledge the need for forms of popular culture, such as film and television, to be critically evaluated and studied at a serious level. It is a publication which ought to have the standing of *The Uses of Literacy* or *Culture and Society*.[20] Yet it remains a rather obscure work despite proving to be massively influential on film education in Britain and Cultural Studies as an academic subject. It developed a style of cultural criticism which dislodged popular culture from the swamp of elitist despair. The forms of popular culture depicted in the book are refracted as a very much living culture rooted in the present and less haunted by, if not entirely extracted from, Leavisite nostalgia for vanished folk cultures and organic societies. Stuart Hall suggested later the book's tentative steps away from Leavis was more strategic than reflective of a genuine engagement with Leavis, as the authors did not want to disengage themselves from the 'strong influence of Leavis among English teachers'. The influence of Leavis is evident in the book's close readings, and the attention to empirical understanding of texts, and both Hall and Whannel had expressed sympathies towards Leavis's methods and aims.[21] The clarity of the book's critique and objectives remain evident: it is a text which singularly aims to encourage discrimination within the emerging field of popular culture. While expressing their gratitude to Hoggart and Williams, Hall and Whannel chart new territory in refusing to dismiss popular culture as second-rate and offering strategies for teaching film, particularly the Western, as directed by John Ford – one of Whannel's consistent passions – in the classroom.

*The Popular Arts* was received in the media as out of touch, even a bit square. *The New Statesman* and the *Spectator* effectively jeered at the book, sneering at the moral tone of its criticism. Eric Hobsbawm, writing in the *Times Literary Supplement*, reviewed the book with cautious optimism indicating that the 'industrialisation of culture' was too much for the authors to fully get to grips with, while Jonathan Miller, editor of the BBC arts show *Monitor* and writing in the *Observer*, was less circumspect in his criticisms, dismissing Hall and Whannel as incapable of developing 'enough concentration to stop bathos

20 Stuart Hall and Paddy Whannel, *The Popular Arts*, first edition, (London: Hutchinson Education, 1964).

21 'What the cinema needs … is a Leavis', insisted Whannel in his article 'Towards a Positive Criticism of the Mass Media', *Film Teacher*, 17 (May 1959): pp. 28–30.

from getting the upper hand' while admitting that the book does 'hover' with a 'good-hearted decency, between a rather diluted Orwellian belles-lettrism and the over-familiar pieties of Richard Hoggart and Raymond Williams'. 'It seems likely,' said Miller as he twisted the knife, 'that the way in which we use our five senses to frame our feelings and opinions is undergoing a radical change. Vision is receiving an unprecedented emphasis … [but] things have moved on.' Philip Oakes, writing in the *Sunday Telegraph*, was one of the few contemporary reviewers in Britain to praise the publication, declaring it 'a witty, acute, sometimes devastating survey of the powerful influences which help to shape all our lives. Possibly it is the most important work in its field since *The Uses of Literacy*.' The book also appears to have a limited circulation either outside histories of cultural studies or outside histories of Stuart Hall's oeuvre. This is a shame as the role of Whannel is overlooked, relegated to a lesser role in light of Hall's subsequent fame as a doyen of cultural studies. 'When I first read *The Popular Arts*,' says Richard Dyer who wrote the introduction to the 2018 re-issue of the book, 'it was very much written by Paddy and Stuart. Stuart Hall was not *Stuart Hall* then! But in a way, as the BFI Education Department increasingly developed, it is very much linked to *The Popular Arts* and that idea of the critical – not in a sense of it being good or bad – engagement with film in that case. *The Popular Arts* was the first [publication] to give a proper account of the popular arts and thinking about how different kinds of interpretation. All of that is there in that book.'[22]

*The Popular Arts* was undeniably a collaboration between Hall and Whannel, but Garry Whannel, Paddy's son, owns a version of the book which belonged to his father, with individual sections highlighted with either 'PW' or 'SH' initials. From this guide, we can ascertain that Whannel was responsible for sole authorship of the chapters entitled 'The Media and Society', 'The Young Audience', 'The Institutions', 'Mass Society: Critics and Defenders' and 'The Curriculum and the Popular Arts'. These chapters provide the genesis for the work of the BFI Education Department over the coming decades. Whannel's chapters, in particular, provide a tentative theory for the understanding of contemporary popular culture emerging from both Britain and America.

[22] Richard Dyer, personal interview, 27 July 2023.

In the chapter titled 'The Media and Society', Whannel reflects on the influence of F. R. Leavis on the BFI Education Department. He claims that

> the divorce between art and life is often reflected in school as a distinction between the 'work' subjects ... and the 'recreative subjects' which prepare us for our leisure time and in which the emphasis is on 'creativity' and 'appreciation.' The arts come to be regarded as sugar on the pill, relegated to the fringes of our lives, rather than as essential ways in which we can articulate experiences. Good Taste is acquired as an additional accomplishment in a kind of finishing-school process once the business of understanding the real world has been completed. This is the well-rounded-man view of culture which always involves the separation of moral values from what are called the aesthetic qualities.[23]

Whannel's position is situated halfway between Leavis and post-Leavisite concerns, and still soldered on to the critical apparatus that literary studies provided. But *The Popular Arts* truly innovates in introducing the aesthetic into cultural analysis, producing a roadmap for film studies to come into closer view. In this sense, it is an Ur-text, tackling film in a rigorous manner hitherto absent from existing critical evaluations of film. Whannel's chapters bring the work of John Ford and genre studies of the Western into the rubric of serious cultural analysis – and into the purview of the BFI Education Department. Whannel skilfully positions his thinking in a manner which removes itself from film appreciation: *The Popular Arts* moves beyond a dilettante approach and instead sets the terms from which a more serious study of film could emerge, pointing towards a critical modernism, and striking openness to American culture, which differentiated his work from Leavis, Hoggart and Williams. Furthermore, *The Popular Arts* was emphatically pedagogical and retained a clarity of expression which remains illuminating even now. Whannel's work on the Western is particularly strong, summoning the genre from critical disrepute and providing it with a form of institutional legitimacy – which was to be further bolstered by the option to study the Western as part of BFI Education Department's extra-mural classes at the University of London.

[23] Hall and Whannel, *The Popular Arts*, pp. 28–9.

From our perspective, the most important chapter of *The Popular Arts* is the final chapter, titled 'The Curriculum and the Popular Arts'. This chapter was inexplicably removed from the most recent editions of the book which feels like a travesty as it provides the clearest demonstration of Whannel's vision for film education. This feels like a travesty as this segment provides the clearest demonstration of Whannel's views on how film ought to be taught through the BFI. The chapter also provides a remarkable delineation of Whannel's wonderful capacity to align theoretical engagement, however naive at this point, with a genuine sense of practical implementation. It situates the current state of film pedagogy within the contexts of the Newsom Report of 1963, which Whannel quotes as highlighting the 'considerable demand that the curriculum be made more "realistic" and "practical"'.[24] Echoing concerns made in the first chapter, Whannel offers a powerful articulation of his position, operating both within and outside Leavisite concerns, insisting that

> the power to discriminate is the power to analyse and evaluate our experiences ... A great deal of teaching in the arts is still taste-changing. Much of it is carried out with the best of intentions, but however worthy the motive, however admirable the standards, it is still of course imposition ... there are standards, but they cannot be imposed, only discovered. It is the teacher's task to assist that discovery, to make individual growth possible. Such an aim implies certain methods.[25]

While these methods are not specified, by questioning the role and function of 'taste' within film pedagogy, Whannel casts the remit of film studies into new, productively undefined, territories. Further quoting from the Newsom Report, he recommends that 'in a very large field of popular culture ... pupils can learn, with guidance, to sharpen their perceptions'. The chapter ends with two recommendations: a full-time course in popular culture, lasting a year which would produce a minority of experts who could continue teaching in their own locality; and, presciently, the establishment of a permanent study laboratory with a staff of four lecturers, each with a different bias, accommodated in a residential building for twelve to eighteen students with a book and film library and a cinema/theatre equipped with both 16mm and 35mm projectors. This

[24] Ibid., p. 389.
[25] Ibid., pp. 391–2.

laboratory would have three functions: firstly, teaching; secondly, servicing the local community in league with the local Adult Education authority and present 'cinema, jazz and folk-music'; and thirdly, provide a centre for research and study. This aspect would consider the work of

> sociologists and psychologists but would place its emphasis on developing critical methods, and it particular it would explore the no-man's land that at present exists between mass-media research and criticism. It would try to establish what contribution might be made by the disciplines of criticism to, say, content analyses where the techniques of research are disturbingly clumsy. Clearly, anyone engaged in probing the relationship between the media and the audience should not only be skilled in the methods of research but also sensitive to the way a medium works as art. We are still at the stage of evolving, for example, the language for handling the complexities of film art. What we need now are studies in depth: detailed analyses of particular films, TV programmes, etc., alongside equally considered examinations of individual response studied over a long period. Research could also be carried out into methods of training appreciation and discrimination with a view to finding out which are the most effective. The study laboratory would provide a much-needed centre for developing work in teaching and criticism.[26]

With this conclusion, Whannel sets out a thrilling set of parameters for a transnational field of cultural criticism operating within an intellectual climate which is open to investigating art forms from across the spectrum of contemporary media. While the development of the Centre for Contemporary Cultural Studies in Birmingham was beginning to partly fulfil these aims, Whannel is also pointing towards a re-calibration of film pedagogy, marking out the BFI Education Department as receptive cultural terrain for critical thinking and intellectually progressive ideas to take root.

*The Popular Arts*'s pedagogical function extended beyond the classroom. While it served as the base text for the serious study of film in Britain, it also provided a culmination to Whannel's writings and conference interventions, serving as a significant statement of his New Left allegiances. *The Popular Arts* became the 'bible' of a generation of aspiring film teachers. Its promotion of authorship, genre, and Hollywood cinema was as much a political act as it was an aesthetic act as it endorsed the taste of the working

[26] Ibid., p. 400.

classes. It was the first book published in Britain to apply a theoretical approach to film, a discipline which had little to no academic standing. From a contemporary perspective, it is arguably more fertile than Hoggart's *The Uses of Literacy* in that it develops and legitimises working-class taste in a far more egalitarian and relatable manner. It also provided a manifesto of sorts for Whannel's vision of what the BFI Education Department could become, as evidenced in that final chapter which provides the basis for a re-imagining of cultural institutions as laboratories for ideas and concepts, a vision which was to inspire and antagonise the BFI for the remainder of the decade.

## The BFI's education outreach

By the time of the publication of *The Popular Arts* in 1964, Whannel had been in post for a number of years and the Education Department was significantly increasing its outreach across Britain. The institute's annual reports tell a story of increased demand for lectures on film and increased pressures on the Education Department to deliver. During 1960–1 alone, the Education Department arranged 641 lectures on film across Britain, 231 of which were given by Whannel and his colleagues.[27] These lectures formed the basis of courses in film, often lasting up to twenty-four weeks, and were primarily provided to university departments of Adult Education, Institutes of Education, Training Colleges, Colleges of Science and Technology, evening institutes, education authorities and local film societies. Within two years, the number of lectures provided by the department reached almost one thousand.[28] One of the main attractions, and biggest undertakings of the Education Department were the BFI Summer Schools which allowed the BFI Education Department to fully flex its outreach ambitions. While we will return in more detail to the summer schools, it is worth noting the innovation in the school's programming after Whannel took over their operation. For example, the 1962 edition, held at St. Andrews in Scotland, attracted eighty students, and guest

[27] British Film Institute, *Twenty-Eighth Annual General Report* (London: BFI, 1961).
[28] British Film Institute, *Thirtieth Annual General Report* (London: BFI, 1963).

LECTURES

JANUARY 1961

**Figure 4** Lecture Programme, January–February 1961, British Film Institute Quarterly Gazette, Winter 1960–1.

speakers included director John Schlesinger, Guy Brenton and Sidney Cole; an Easter School was also held at Bede College in Durham with Paddy Whannel, Stuart Hall and Roy Knight as lecturers.[29] The list of courses remains quite an exciting insight into the department's concerns at the time: French Cinema and the French avant-garde; Film Language movement; Humphrey Jennings's documentaries and the Free Cinema movement, with extra lectures on the contemporary work of Karel Reisz and Tony Richardson were all covered over the course of the weekend. It is also important to attest to the department's work outside of London and its importance for disseminating film education to places and people who may not have had the opportunity to see films or

[29] One of these attendees was Colin MacArthur who was later to play an important role in the BFI until the mid-1980s. Laura Mulvey also recalled that 'Paddy Whannel played golf and because he was a working-class Scot, he didn't see golf as belonging to middle classes. That's why the BFI Summer Schools were often held at St. Andrews – it was near the golf course!' Laura Mulvey, personal interview, 6 November 2023.

**Figure 5** Film Teaching manual. BFI Education Department.

engage with other film enthusiasts. Yet the department funds were clearly stretched, and Whannel reported a great strain on resources as the department was increasingly called upon to provide advice and help to an overwhelming number of lecturers and teachers across the country who were attempting to work with film but required advice and guidance on simply how to use film in the classroom. Whannel pointed to a wider need for more extracts from feature films, and greater documentation recording the experiences of those working with film on 'flourishing courses' being provided by the Education Department.[30]

These difficulties were made even more explicit in the Education Department pamphlet entitled *Film Teaching*, which we briefly mentioned earlier, and was published in 1964, the same year as *The Popular Arts*.[31] In the opening essay, Stuart Hall, then a lecturer in film and media at the Chelsea College of

[30] British Film Institute, *Thirtieth Annual General Report* (London: BFI, 1963).
[31] Stuart Hall, Albert Hunt, Roy Knight and Alan Lovell, *Film Teaching* (London: BFI Education Department, 1964).

Science and Technology, describes the absurd difficulties facing a film teacher developing a course under the wide rubric of the liberal arts, which already exists on the margins of the curriculum in a technology college attended by student chemists studying for a science diploma. In a separate essay, Albert Hunt, an area tutor organiser for Shropshire Education Committee, also details the post-screening discussions in remote communities responding to Satyajit Ray's *The World of Apu* (1959) while Alan Lovell details the curriculum of a two-year course of film study offered by the University of London's Extra-Mural Department and supported by the BFI. By the time this pamphlet was being disseminated around the country, Stuart Hall had left his role at Chelsea College, and his adjunct roles at the BFI, to work with Richard Hoggart at the Centre for Contemporary Culture Studies in Birmingham. But *Film Teaching* and *The Popular Arts* contributed to creating publishing conditions which allowed for books on films to emerge, even more so for more rigorous analyses of popular culture could be disseminated. While Hall and Hoggart took this in a different direction in Birmingham with a focus on more sociological analysis of culture, Whannel maintained his own visions for the study of culture at the BFI Education Department and it was during this period in the early- to mid-1960s when the pragmatism of Whannel's approach began to fully take shape. Whether one adhered to the Leavisite views on the traditions of high culture or went in a different direction and allowed for the student to develop their own individual responses, the critical position at the centre of both responses was undeniable and formed the fulcrum of these innovative initiatives. Objective knowledge of the objects under consideration was the solution and, in Whannel's view, it was one which could be shared by both teacher and student.

But the key figures in the Education Department at the time continued to tour the country giving film lectures. David Lusted, later a key member of the BFI Education Department, remembers Paddy Whannel coming to give a talk at Bulmershe College in Reading around this time. Whannel showed *Wagon Master*, directed by John Ford, to the college's film society – which at that point had preferred world cinema to Westerns.[32] Yet Whannel's presentation was mesmerising and transformed Lusted's view of film and inspired him to teach

32 David Lusted, personal interview, 31 March 2023.

his own film course to teenagers. Whannel subsequently asked Lusted to write an advisory document about the course which led to Lusted joining SEFT and later BFI Education Department. Indeed, this work traversing the country, giving lectures on film was also increasingly supported by SEFT. Whannel had made an alliance between the two institutions, and the two organisations liaised with regard to resources without interrupting the independence of each other. Journals were key in this collaboration and SEFT members received *Screen Education* journal six times a year. *Screen Education* still maintained a primarily informative role, offering updates to teachers working with film on work being done in the field at a national level along with reference information on film extract availability, a film distribution directory and a modicum of film reviews and interviews. SEFT had its own summer school, separate to the BFI Summer Schools, but similar in format: a fortnight spent examining the background to film teaching through critical lectures, seminars on teaching practice and viewing sessions. But SEFT was generally seen as the more stuffy, old-fashioned counterpart to the more progressive work being undertaken at the BFI Education Department. There was a split between the practical needs of the teachers working at local levels across the country and the more expansive aims of the BFI Education Department with Whannel's aims to craft laboratories for the study of film. This split was to mark the work of both institutions, despite their working in tandem, throughout the following decades. David Lusted recalls this in detail.

> I'd just started teaching in the late 1960s when Roger Watkins, a formative mentor at a new liberal educational teacher-training college in Berkshire, helped me compose the first CSE course in Film Studies for a 15+ age group in my school. This brought me into the orbit of BFI Education, its staff led by the pioneering Head, Paddy Whannel. These two figures were responsible for me joining SEF (The Society for Education in Film, as it then was: the T for TV came later) and then its committee. BFI Education was at that time leading a movement to establish Film Studies as an intellectual discipline, together with founding film education in schools and colleges. SEF was a teachers' organisation promoting what it called film appreciation, though it was interested more in schools filmmaking (cine was the medium of the times). In my relatively youthful naivety, I found the experience of SEF monthly committee meetings alienating. It was a shock to find a teachers' organisation representing a modern arts subject like film dominated by an older generation

> of educational traditionalists, many surprisingly teachers of geography rather than humanities subjects as I'd expected, here and there sporting leather patches on the elbows of their jackets, and almost all pipe-smoking. When I said something like I think SEF should concern itself not just about the 'great and worthy' of film history but also about popular cinema, I'll never forget the putdown I got. When I mentioned this to Paddy, he said that it was my responsibility to change that, to ally with committee members more like me. When I said, 'I don't know any like me', he said, 'then come on our courses and meet some'. In those days, there were no degree courses in film. The only way to obtain a film qualification of any kind back then was from the University of London and BFI extra-mural course, a three-year certificate and a fourth-year diploma course that was just starting up. I joined, where I did indeed find like-minded people. It was a transformative experience.[33]

By the point in the early to mid-1960s, the BFI Education Department had found great interest and success with their extra-mural courses on film with the University of London. Alan Lovell provided four of the most popular courses: Realism and the Cinema, The Anarchist Cinema, Qualities of Film, and Renoir and the French Cinema. The primary issue for teaching film at this point was the availability of film extracts and the paucity of literature on contemporary film aside from the magazines and journals. But there was a positive aspect to this. The Education Department's work was not burdened by the fear of simply popularising other people's ideas. The department's work was pioneering because the lecturers and students were not overwhelmed by existing scholarship. The extra-mural classes relished the informality of the discourse which, by all accounts, was very rewarding for lecturers and students alike. Indeed, the only existing scholarship on film was, in fact, to be found in *Sight and Sound* and the proliferation of magazines and journals emerging from Oxford and Cambridge.

## Film criticism and film education

The way in which the development of film education and film criticism were intimately connected is illustrated by the blurring of boundaries between the two. Since the era of Stanley Reed, much of the BFI Education Department's

[33] David Lusted, personal interview, 31 March 2023.

work was concentrated on writing and publishing, and it is striking to note how many of the Education Department's staff were also film journalists, before, during and after their time working for the institute. While the BFI's extra-mural classes were relishing the freedom of working with film in the classroom, film criticism had become a site of struggle both in France and Britain in the late 1950s and early 1960s. The influence of the British documentary movement had also influenced criticism, particularly *Sight and Sound*, the BFI's own magazine, and journals and magazines such as the *Penguin Film Review*, *Sequence* and *Definition*. These outlets largely favoured realism as a counterpoint to the excess of Hollywood glamour while social documentaries, as per the work of John Grierson, were favoured over the fantasies of Westerns. These social documentaries were linked, in Britain at least, with those concepts of the artisan, the craftsman, the individual creator. These ideas merged, particularly from *Sequence* magazine, to form the Free Cinema movement which took working-class communities, often in the north of England, as their primary subject matter. The films emerging from this movement were noticeably more permissive about language and risqué content and offered a naturalistic, even journalistic, style of presentation. The movement was cemented through six programmes screening at the NFT from 1956 through 1958. The primary directors involved, including Lindsay Anderson, Karel Reisz and Tony Richardson, shared concerns with Hoggart and Williams around the culture of life within communities, the negative effects of mass-media, but also stood within a contemporary tradition of working-class dissenting art in the vein of Alan Sillitoe and John Osborne.

Meanwhile, in Paris, a set of entirely different forces were shaping their own take on contemporary film. The combination of the Vichy regime, German occupation and the banning of American films during the war period resulted in the foundation of illicit ciné-clubs across France – one notable enterprise was run by André Bazin, founder of *Cahiers du Cinéma* – which showed these films, while after the war, Americans and American films were re-cast as great liberating forces of both politics and culture.[34] The French

[34] See Peter Matthews, 'Diving the Real: The Leaps of Faith in André Bazin's Film Criticism', https://2.bfi.org.uk/news-opinion/sight-sound-magazine/features/andre-bazin-divining-real-film-criticism-overview, accessed 10 June 2024.

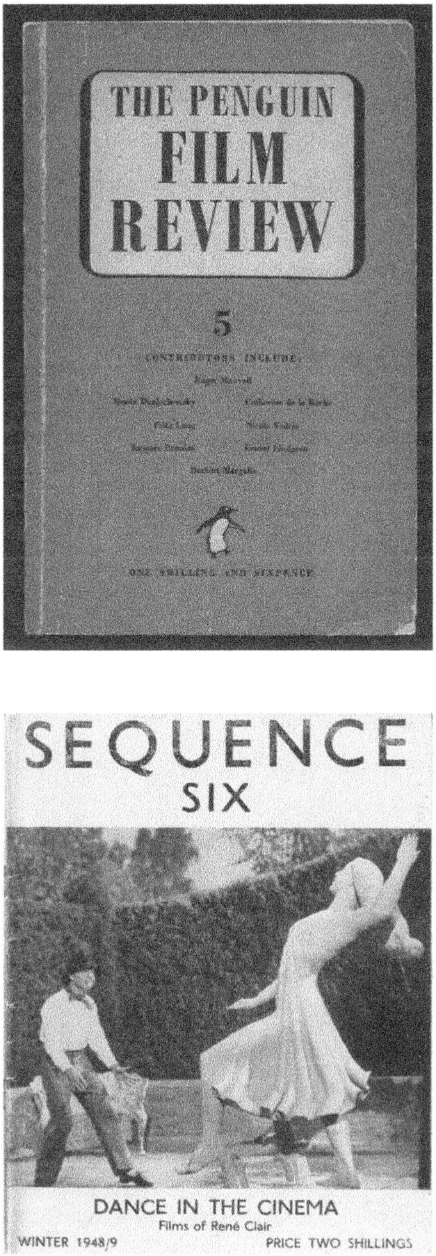


**Figure 6a and 6b** *The Penguin Film Review* and *Sequence* film journals.

enthusiasm for American literature, especially William Faulkner, further emboldened this adoption of American culture as both compelling and necessary. The more outré aspects of Hollywood dream and fantasy film, the pulp of horror and B-movies, and the eye-popping visuals of vamps and pin-ups were inculcated into a culture already loosened up through the French surrealist tradition. It was within this climate which *Cahiers du Cinéma* was founded. It was concurrent with a form of thinking and writing about film which was a striking counterpoint to the more traditional concerns of social cinema and Free Cinema in Britain. It was the second wave of critics from *Cahiers du Cinéma* which formulated the auteur theory which came to dominate film education, through both teaching and writing at the BFI Education Department throughout the 1960s and early 1970s. The auteur theory strived to recognise film directors in the same way novels recognise their authors. The definition of auteur theory, according to Andrew Sarris, was that a film-maker's individual style and complete control over all elements of production give a film its personal and unique stamp.[35] Perhaps, the primary beneficiary of this new approach was the director Howard Hawks. Hawks had been steadily making film since the 1920s, but his work, perhaps due to its sheer diversity, had never been looked at as a whole. Auteur theory allowed for an analysis of Hawks's entire oeuvre, revealing a pattern of distinct themes and motifs. While the *Cahiers* critics deployed auteur theory to shift their critical focus entirely towards a number of French directors – Jean Renoir, Robert Bresson, Jean Cocteau, Jacques Becker, Abel Gance, Max Ophuls, Jacques Tati and Roger Leenhard – the theory, which was re-calibrated as the *politique des auteurs*, was soon mobilised to critically re-evaluate a whole group of American film directors, many of whom were relatively obscure within America itself. Auteur theory would prove to be deeply important for much of the work undertaken by the BFI Education Department and *Screen* journal, in that it provided a rationale for accepting commercial cinema, taking as given that a film is made for an audience and is a representation of the director's desire to engage with others.

[35] See Andrew Sarris, 'Notes on the Auteur Theory in 1962', *Film Culture* 27, nos. 1–8 (Winter 1962–3): 1–8.

**Figure 7** *Oxford Opinion* film journal, 1960 issue.

The influence of auteur theory was much felt at Oxford in the early 1960s. Film societies had become key sites for the development of film criticism, birthing a number of highly influential publications. *Oxford Opinion* and its later offshoot *Movie* were launched as vehicles for the promotion of auteurist concepts. This was an ambitious, contrarian project from the off: the first issue of *Movie* provided a histogram listing 204 directors, from Britain and America, and categorising them under six headings: 'Great', 'Brilliant', 'Very Talented', 'Talented', 'Competent or Ambitious' and 'The Rest'. Most of the British directors in the list are in the 'Competent or Ambitious' section and it appears that the function of the histogram is to highlight the sheer inferiority of British cinema in comparison to its American counterparts. In fact, the two highest rated British film-makers are not British at all: Joseph Losey, who had been blacklisted in Hollywood under McCarthyism; and Hugo Fregonese, an Argentinian-born director whose meagre connection to British cinema were two films shot in Britain in the late 1950s. Alfred

Hitchcock is firmly placed as 'Great' but is on the American side – favouring his American output as opposed to his earlier British films.[36] Behind this disparaging view of British film lay a rejection of the social realism and documentary movements, in favour of an embrace of Hollywood. Perkins's article was the first public articulation of this shift in focus, but it was an outlook shared by many of the burgeoning film critics and educators circling the BFI at the time.

*Movie* firmly placed itself at an obtuse angle to the work of *Sight and Sound*. By the early 1950s, *Sight and Sound* was largely taken over by the writers and film-makers from *Sequence* magazine, including Lindsay Anderson, Karel Reisz and Gavin Lambert, who later formed the Free Cinema movement and were supported by the magazine's long-term editor Penelope Houston, a pioneering figure in her own right as female editor of a film magazine. Houston succeeded in steering *Sight and Sound* into a generally left-wing approach to film criticism, valuing terms such as commitment and evaluation over the form of critical analysis practiced by Hall and Whannel in *The Popular Arts*. Meanwhile, copies of *Cahiers du Cinéma* were being brought back from Paris and feverishly read at Oxford. Ian Cameron introduced the magazine to Victor Perkins and Alan Lovell at Oxford – *Sight and Sound*, at this point, was the 'posh end of British film criticism', in Perkins's terms. Cahiers was positioned in opposition, along with other oddities such as Ado Kyrou's *Amour-Erotisme et Cinema*, which offered a different ideological slant to *Cahiers* with a robust set of critical values, including a highly intemperate takedown of David Lean's *Brief Encounter* – this made a particular impression on Perkins's own critical stance.[37]

Another important influence were the MacMahonists, a vociferous bunch of film critics founded by Pierre Rissient in the late 1950s and based at the Cinema MacMahon, on the Avenue MacMahon in full view of the Arc de Triomphe. The MacMahonists published *Presence du cinema* and visited

[36] Victor Perkins, 'The British Cinema', *Movie*, 1962 (London, May 1962), reprinted in Douglas Pye, ed., *V. F. Perkins on Movies* (Detroit: Wayne State University Press, 2020), p. 34. Perkins was to join the BFI Education Department in early 1966.

[37] See John Gibbs, 'Interviews: Ian Cameron, V.F. Perkins, Charles Barr, Alan Lovell – Combined Interviews', https://centaur.reading.ac.uk/84433/1/Combined%20interviews.pdf, accessed 11 May 2024.

London in the early 1960s, encountering the *Oxford Opinion* writers and making a particular impression on Ian Cameron.[38] Anticipating an outright hostility to English culture which would later mark both the *New Left Review* and the BFI Education Department, the work undertaken by the *Oxford Opinion* group represented an almost gleeful rejection of anything considered British. Furthermore, all of these figures – including their contemporary Peter Wollen, who was soon to play an important role across these networks – were operating in a university system where there were no established curricula or syllabi for the study of film. This was quite freeing as it allowed film criticism, even on an amateur level, to flourish without the influence of any official creed – in fact, *Sight and Sound* was probably the closest thing to an authority at the time that it represented a rather old-fashioned form of middle-class taste. Film had its own nascent culture, and it was undisciplined, which allowed these magazines to emerge and an entirely fresh discourse to emerge alongside. The film clubs and societies of the universities offered space for discussion and analysis and for cadres to be formed. The social life of film analysis and criticism, certainly at Oxbridge, was vibrant and healthy. The critical emergence of *Oxford Opinion* and *Movie*, in tandem with *The Popular Arts*, was crucial in moving film criticism into a more robust form in that the writing about film was informed, lucid and pugnacious, especially when considered in contrast to earlier publications such as Roger Manvell's *The Art of Film*. A link emerged between these writers and the *Cahiers du Cinéma* editors: Robin Wood wrote a serious piece on Alfred Hitchcock's *Psycho*, sent it to Penelope Houston who was now editing *Sight and Sound* who rejected it because she felt *Psycho* was ultimately 'a joke'. However, Wood had the temerity to send it to *Cahiers* who soon published his piece as a lead article in the magazine.[39] These magazines became signatures of modernity within film criticism, where *Sight and Sound* was making no such appeals and was quite vulnerable to their criticisms.

In 1960, Penelope Houston wrote an article entitled 'The Critical Question', for *Sight and Sound*. The article points to the uneven

38 Ibid.

39 Ibid.

development of left-criticism in Britain; it points to developments such as Joan Littlewood's Theatre Workshops, *Universities and Left Review*, the Aldermaston marches, along with Sequence magazine and *Sight and Sound*'s own publishing of articles by Lindsay Anderson, as indicative of 'committed' criticism. However, Houston insists that the greatest danger to this form of criticism lies from within those who 'carry its banner'. Houston places the blame at *Cahiers du Cinema*, dismissing its analyses as 'a series of slightly breathless statements' and insisting that cinema is 'entitled to the kind of critical analysis that has traditionally been devoted to the theatre and the novel ...cinema is about the human situation, not about spatial relationships'.[40] Houston's criteria for criticism, humanist in approach, failed to persuade the new wave of film critics. Charles Barr at *Granta*, Raymond Durgnat in *Motion* and Robin Wood writing in *Definition* argued vehemently against Houston, with Wood raging that 'the content of a book isn't a synopsis of its plot. Its content is the words of which it is composed; change them, and you have not only changed the style but changed the content. And how much less is a film a synopsis of its plot, or its author's noble intentions! The content of a film is moving images, words, and sounds, fused into a unity.'[41]

Houston's article, however, does make an important point. 'The Young Left,' she opines, 'which has found its Osbornes and Weskers, its Bergers and Tynans, has yet to find its politicians.' Without representation on a political level, these writers and cineaste on the left had to find alternative means of impacting upon and modernising the structures of culture in 1960s Britain. The BFI benefitted from this, particularly its Education Department, in that it provided the means for intellectuals on the left to make interventions in the way in which we conceive of film. Paddy Whannel was in the position of being plugged into developments on the cultural left and able to employ many of these film critics writing so eloquently against *Sight and Sound* – which, as we know, was also a BFI publication.

[40] Penelope Houston, 'The Critical Question', *Sight and Sound*, 29, no. 4 (Autumn 1960): pp. 160–5.
[41] Robin Wood, 'New Criticism?', *Definition*, no. 3 (Winter 1960–1): pp. 9–11.

**Figure 8a and 8b** 'The Critical Question', *Sight and Sound*, Autumn 1960.

## The formation of film and theory

In 1960, the *Universities and Left Review* and *New Reasoner* had merged to form the *New Left Review*, edited by Stuart Hall. By the end of the following year, the journal was in financial crisis and Perry Anderson, an Anglo-Irish writer and historian who had attended Eton and Oxford assumed full control of the journal by early 1963. Anderson wanted to open up the *New Left Review* beyond what he saw as the complacency and parochial vision of its previous iteration.[42] This pointed the journal in the direction of Western Marxism and what we now call the Global South but was then referred to as the Third World. But there was a third way: the *New Left Review* shifted its cultural axis in the form of a regular 'Motifs' section which was to be edited by Peter Wollen, who had attended Oxford with Anderson. Having deserted from National Service in the British Army, Wollen was on the run and wrote for the *NLR* under two pseudonyms: Lee Russell and Lucien Rey. As editor of 'Motifs', Wollen commissioned himself to write a series of thumbnail sketches on film directors. He also commissioned his friend Alan Beckett to write about jazz and pop music. Wollen was working in parallel to Whannel in pioneering a form of criticism indebted to both Hollywood and jazz, although the two men had not met yet. But the 'Motifs' section was specifically in dialogue with the Western Marxism of the *New Left Review*; the journal presented an array of subjects which was rare in aligning pieces on Lucien Goldmann and Ernest Mendel alongside Hollywood directors such as Nicholas Ray and Sam Fuller. This juxtaposition of concepts was to prove influential for Wollen, who was already under the spell of the American film critic Eugene Archer, a friend of the journalist Andrew Sarris who had defined the auteur theory.[43] There

42 Perry Anderson, *Arguments within English Marxism* (London: New Left Books, 1979), pp. 147–9. For Anderson's reflections on the actual transfer of editorial control of the *New Left Review* in 1962–3, rejecting the notion of a coup as a 'legend', see pp. 135–7 (a more substantial account than that provided in 'Statement', *NLR*, no. 24 (March–April 1964): p. 112). Some more personal thoughts can be found in Anderson's obituary 'Diary' on Edward Thompson, *London Review of Books* (21 October 1993): pp. 24–5. For a counter viewpoint, in 'a voice choking with anger', see E. P. Thompson's 'The Peculiarities of the English', *Socialist Register*, 1965, which provides both a history and a denunciation of the Anderson takeover of the *New Left Review*.

43 'There were a couple of people who were extremely influential on Peter's career in his early days but, as they didn't actually write, they get forgotten. One of these was Eugene [Gene] Archer whom he met through his Oxford friend Patrick Bauchau. Gene had been the *New York Times* film critic, but something went wrong, he lost his job, went to Paris, where he met Patrick. Their friendship was

was an increasingly explicit dismissal, in the *New Left Review* and in the aforementioned film criticism from Oxford, of anything considered English. This Oedipal rejection, as termed by Laura Mulvey who was in a personal and creative relationship with Wollen throughout the 1960s and 1970s, caused some tension.

> In a sense, the previous generation [of left culture] were kicked out – E.P. Thompson and Raymond Williams. I want to triangulate the rejection of Englishness – the openness to American popular culture and European ideas – and that was very strong for Peter Wollen. He started writing for the *NLR* on that wave, first through his Iran pieces which fitted in with their focus upon [the Global South]. Roger Murray on Africa and Peter's own writings were bringing neo-colonialism into leftist discourse. But Peter had an in-depth journalistic side, and he had a Hollywood side. He was also living in Rome and working for the *International Socialist* journal. Paddy read his *New Left Review* articles and was fascinated. Paddy was already collecting together his gang. Alan Lovell was already there. And that built up the numbers.[44]

From 1962 to 1965, Peter Wollen, under the pseudonym of Lee Russell, wrote nine portraits of film directors for the *NLR*: Nicholas Ray, Sam Fuller, Budd Boetticher, Alfred Hitchcock, Jean Renoir, Howard Hawks, Roberto Rossellini, Josef von Sternberg and Louis Malle. None of the directors he chose to write about was British, aside from Alfred Hitchcock, whose work as a director in Britain was dismissed by Wollen. His inspiration in these thumbnail sketches was the *politique des auteurs* as practiced by *Cahiers du Cinéma*: mapping Hollywood cinema in a rigorous fashion and developing readings in the aesthetics of films. There was also a rewriting of the Anglophone film canon.

based on, or cemented by, their mutual passion for the great Hollywood directors of the studio system period – as, indeed, pioneered by the Cahiers du Cinéma. Although it has been said that Andrew Sarris's later American Cinema may have been influenced by Archer and Bachau, but it was Sarris who actually wrote up, and translated into English, this quite revolutionary critical reassessment of Hollywood. I am interested in the way that some people, perhaps really influential intellectuals in their day, become shadowy figures because they didn't write anything to be remembered by. I think Eugene Archer fits into this pattern. Paddy Whannel is somewhat similar. He exerted a really key influence on that generation of young, up and coming film critics and theorists but, most specifically, created an institutional environment that made their subsequent work, and then their influence, evolve. Perhaps our culture undervalues the 'enabler'... It's great that you are going back and researching Paddy's story'. Laura Mulvey, personal interview, 6 November 2023.

44 ibid.

Wollen was eager to write about the aesthetics of movie directors such as Fuller and Boetticher rather than limiting such analysis to the canon of art cinema represented by figures such as Roberto Rossellini or Ingmar Bergman. Wollen also refrained from viewing Hollywood as an amorphous morass of 'mass culture' and clearly differentiated between the works of the various directors.

Peter Wollen took the *politique des auteurs* method and comprehensively reinvented it through his readings of Western Marxist texts simultaneously being published in the *New Left Review*. The innovation of this construction does not simply lie in the combining of two distinctive methods of analysis. It lies, more essentially, in the powerful assertions of substantive argument around film. 'The *politique* was brought to American by Eugene Archer and Andrew Sarris,' reflected Wollen in 1988, 'popularised in Britain by *Movie* magazine. The problem with it, as far as I was concerned, was that it was not truly an auteur theory. It was not really theoretical.'[45] This confluence of theory and film was the product of two distinct bodies of writing which, under Wollen's sophisticated prose, bevelled smoothly together to form a body of work which comprehensively breaks with the orthodoxy of film criticism and education. Film had long been a discipline in search of a theory to scaffold its claims to be a subject worthy of serious study. We will see shortly how Wollen's work was to provide enormous gain for the BFI Education Department. No other film critic in the Anglophone world saw film's need for theory as clearly as Wollen nor was anyone working with film and theory in such an eloquent manner.

In essence, Wollen was a theorist in search of a 'theory' to underpin his writings on film. And he found such a theory, for a brief period at least, through the work of the Romanian French sociologist and literary critic Lucien Goldmann. Wollen deployed concepts from Goldmann's work in his thumbnail sketches for the *New Left Review*, making film like a language, a system, even a structure analysable in and of itself. But his allegiance to Goldmann did not last. Wollen said in 1997:

> Structuralism and semiology hit Britain in a big way through Claude Lévi-Strauss and Roland Barthes. Barthes' *Elements of Semiology* swept me off my feet when I read it first in French in [the journal] *Communications*,

[45] Peter Wollen, 'Thinking Theory', *Film Comment* 24, no. 4 (July–August 1988): pp. 50–1.

and then when it came out in translation as a Jonathan Cape pocketbook. Barthes was still a militant structuralist and so I naturally turned back to reread Lévi-Strauss, who I hadn't looked into since his great ethnographic memoir, *Tristes Tropiques* (A World on the Wane). Rereading Lévi-Strauss, I saw how your work could be configured by using Lévi-Strauss instead of Goldmann.[46]

Wollen deduced similar patterns of identifying recurring motifs in both forms of analyses and created a lineage between this new work and structural analysis in other fields. In parallel to his readings of contemporary Western Marxism, Wollen utilised Vladimir Propp's morphology of folktales which itself was also re-configured by the Belgian-French anthropologist Claude Lévi-Strauss who was developing his own form of structuralism at the same time. Lévi-Straus's work was published in English in the mid-1960s, and reading his work allowed Wollen to consider the semantic dimension of his analyses, confronting the commonalities between all stories, be they films or folktales, as well as their differences.

But Wollen had something significant in common with the writers from *Movie* and *Oxford Opinion* which was, as Laura Mulvey called it, the Oedipal rejection of anything English. Wollen was particularly scathing towards the work of *Sight and Sound*, and in a review of Penelope Houston's *The Contemporary Cinema*, a slimline account of cinema from 1945 to 1963, Wollen aggressively critiques the 'ideology of stupefied traditionalism and empiricism, an anti-ideology which is the enemy of all ideas and all calculation'. Houston is derided as exhibiting 'serene indifference', one that is only shaken when she makes attempts to 'cope with the influence of *Cahiers du Cinéma*'. Accusing Houston of cultural insensitivity, Wollen insists that her 'account of the critical positions and arguments of the *Cahiers* concludes with the old gibe that their enthusiasm for American cinema is partly based on their inability to speak or understand English'. Furthermore, Houston's apparent inability to adapt to the *politique des auteurs* methodology has led her to make 'the most unfortunate judgements on American cinema' and her position is 'impressionist relativism at its worst'. All of this occurs even before Houston

46 Peter Wollen, 'Lee Russell Interviews Peter Wollen', in *Signs and Meaning in the Cinema* (London: BFI, 1997), pp. 211–48. Claude Lévi-Strauss, *Tristes Tropiaues* (Paris: Librairie Plon, 1955); *Tristes Tropiques*, trans. John Russell (London: Hutchinson, 1961).

has the temerity to tackle the French new wave of film-making, whereupon Wollen ridicules her for failing to link Jean-Luc Godard's *À bout de souffle* with the contemporary work of Samuel Fuller. Wollen's indignation reaches a state of apoplexy by the article's close:

> Penelope Houston's fear of theory and ideology, however, reaches even more extreme lengths than failure to understand the critical achievements of Cahiers du Cinéma. It leads to a complete abnegation on her part of any kind of coherent approach to the films she does admire. There is no possibility, it seems, of relating anything meaningful to anything, of applying any useful methodology, of seeming to locate any film in any kind of structure greater than itself, historical sociological or ideological. Films show 'how people behave and give themselves away in action'. Beyond that nothing can be elucidated.[47]

Wollen's article is important as it reflects the clearest articulation of a change in the ideological atmosphere towards film at an institutional level in Britain. It symbolises a doctrine which became a primacy at the BFI Education Department for decades to come. The strength of feeling in Wollen's attack on Houston prompts depth of thinking. Wollen's arguments are startling and original and reflects a desire to overthrow the established order.

While Paddy Whannel's own involvement with the New Left had reduced after the *New Left Review* takeover by Perry Anderson, he was to remain affiliated to these networks. Whannel set about assembling a new team at BFI Education Department from the mid-1960s, and looked to the journals on the left for talented film writers who could become film educators. In January 1966, he appointed Peter Wollen to the role of publications officer, and also appointed Victor Perkins to the role of teacher adviser. Because Whannel's expertise primarily lay in administration, and in helping others to reach their potential, his own role been shrouded in the historical record. But the effect of his work and that of the people he employed at this time was to prove strategically essential for film education in Britain. It also reminds us that innovation, particularly within the constraints of institutions, does not emerge all at once but is the effect of years and decades of work. Whannel had been in

[47] Lee Russell, 'Culture and Cinema', *New Left Review* 1, no. 21 (September–October 1963): pp. 112–14.

position since 1957 – it took almost ten years for his vision for the department to come into focus. As we will see, there is something institutionally and analytically distinct about the work engendered by Whannel and his team. It is strikingly rigorous, intellectually curious and defiantly transnational in outlook.

But it is impossible to separate this innovation impact of increased resources on the institution, which allows for ideas to flourish and circulate in tandem with ease of practical implementation. The Labour government elected in 1964 after thirteen years of Conservative rule would prove to be the first administration to acknowledge film as an art. In late 1963, the Department of Education and Science promised to directly fund the educational work of the BFI. Looking at the BFI's annual reports from this time, the grant appears to be in the region of £20,000 per annum, almost £500,000 in today's money.[48] Plans were immediately put in place to develop a series of publications, the first of which was the aforementioned *Film Teaching*; from 1964 the department also started to work with the Centre for Contemporary Culture Studies at Birmingham, re-uniting Whannel with Stuart Hall and Richard Hoggart, along with plans to develop work with the National Council of Women. The Education Department was moved into an entirely new building on Old Compton Street. New staff members were appointed before the arrival of Wollen and Perkins: Jim Kitses, a Harvard-educated American anthropologist, and Alan Lovell. It is striking now to consider that each of these figures were also sophisticated writers on film, each of whom were to publish influential texts over the course of the following decade. The tenor of the story changes here because much of this counter-energy which we have explored in this chapter, and had been diffused through different journals, was coming together under the banner of the BFI Education Department. What would emerge most influentially was an Education Department devoted to legitimising and modernising film and film education. The support of the Labour government, and in particular Jennie Lee, who took on the newly created role of Minister for the Arts, gave huge impetus to the work undertaken by Whannel and his team. Lee's *A Policy for the Arts – First Steps*, published in 1965, recognised that the arts needed to be embedded in the education system

[48] British Film Institute, *Thirty-First Annual General Report* (BFI: London, 1964).

and allocated the financial resources to make this happen. This impacted upon both the BFI Education Department and the country's art schools, some of which were already teaching film in advance of the traditional curriculum, created the space for appointing innovative, progressively minded people in significant roles at cultural and educational institutions across Britain.[49] Once these people were in post, the ideas and theories they wanted to pursue were immediately disseminated and, later on, the films they wanted to make were being made. This resulted in a remarkable wave of work emerging from the BFI, the art schools and collectives such as Cinema Action, Berwick Street, the London Women's Film Group and many more.[50] The astonishing knock-on effect of institutional support, along with financial resources, which were made available at the time cannot be overstated. Rather than this work being fragmented, as it was during the late 1950s and 1960s, it started to coalesce and ferment into radical new concepts of cinema. The BFI Education Department, flanked by SEFT, was at the centre of these developments, and we will explore this in detail in the following chapter.

[49] The work of Thorold Dickinson at the Slade School of Art was hugely influential. See Henry K. Miller, 'Slade Film School: The Departure That Was Nearly a Movement', *Guardian*, https://www.theguardian.com/film/filmblog/2011/jan/28/slade-film-school-studies-ucl, accessed 10 July 2024.

[50] 'During the 1970s, more money and more institutional support for experimental films became available giving rise to an energetic experimental film culture. The art schools had recently brought film onto the curriculum producing artist film-makers who primarily gathered around the London Filmmakers Co-op. But there were quite a few left collectives like Cinema Action, Berwick Street – who made *Nightcleaners*, for instance. Somewhere in between those left collectives on one end of the spectrum, and the artist films on the other end, experimental narrative had emerged: for instance, Peter and me, and the London Women's Film Group. All these different trends came together in 1974, when the Independent Filmmaker's Association was founded. The IFA fostered a sense of solidarity across these different approaches to radical film. We might be making very different kinds or experimental or radical film, but these different trends could speak to each other and could actually be positive rather than fragmented. All those things made a very rich background for experimental film throughout the 1970s'.

Laura Mulvey, personal interview, 6 November 2023.

2

# Give me a sign

## The BFI Summer Schools

The impact of the dual work of the BFI Education Department and SEFT during the 1960s was formative for film educators. Much of this legacy stems from the manner in which both organisations ran their summer schools and weekend events. While the presentation of these events may seem standard now, the combination of film screenings, lectures and presentations from figures such as Paddy Whannel and Peter Wollen, followed by collective sessions where participants worked in small groups, discussing the films was revolutionary. This was influential, particularly for almost every person I spoke to who worked in and around these institutions at this time.

The summer schools were conceptually and theoretically well ahead of the official realisation of film as a subject at university level. They allowed forms of thinking about film to emerge where insight and expertise formed an alliance with enthusiasm and institutional support. The summer schools also captured a *jejune* form of film education as many of the participants were encountering film for the very first time in an institutional setting. Similarly to the extra-mural courses offered by the Education Department at the time, they enhanced the idea of the institution's operating like a quasi-university through disseminating ideas and facilitating conversation. Ideas were allowed to flourish in a productively ill-disciplined manner. The nature of the summer schools were grounded in collaboration, remote from private study, which provided the engine for this synthesis of presentation, interpretations and debate amid a convivial social setting. These events provide one of the clearest, most deliberate examples of the social life of ideas, and their influence on a generation of film scholars and educators point to the later, parallel effects of reading groups on the women's movement in the 1970s, and to which we will return.

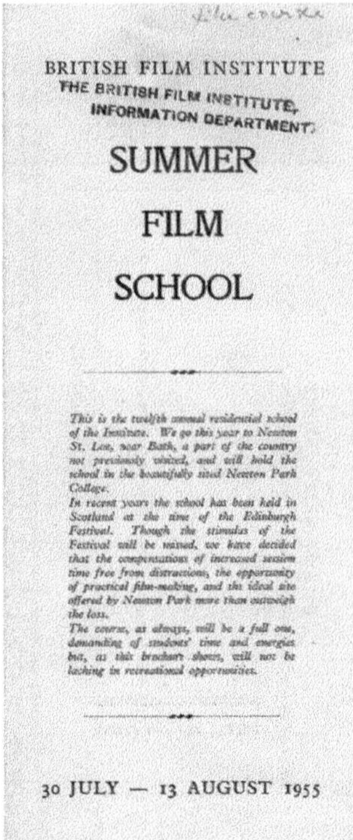
BRITISH FILM INSTITUTE
THE BRITISH FILM INSTITUTE, INFORMATION DEPARTMENT
SUMMER
FILM
SCHOOL
This is the twelfth annual residential school of the Institute. We go this year to Newton St. Loe, near Bath, a part of the country not previously visited, and will hold the school in the beautifully sited Newton Park College.
In recent years the school has been held in Scotland at the time of the Edinburgh Festival. Though the stimulus of the Festival will be missed, we have decided that the compensations of increased session time free from distractions, the opportunity of practical film-making, and the ideal site offered by Newton Park more than outweigh the loss.
The course, as always, will be a full one, demanding of students' time and energies but, as this brochure shows, will not be lacking in recreational opportunities.
30 JULY — 13 AUGUST 1955

British Film Institute
SUMMER SCHOOL 1971
REALISM:
THEORY &
PRACTICE
Eastbourne 31 July - 14 August

BRITISH FILM INSTITUTE
SUMMER SCHOOL 1969
ORMSKIRK 16th-30th August
the FRENCH NEW WAVE

1967
summer film school

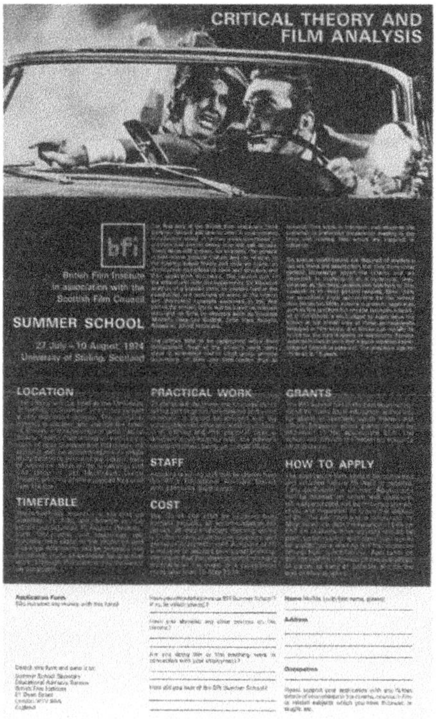


**Figure 9a–9e** BFI Summer School brochures. Courtesy Colin MacArthur.

The origins of the summer schools are also to be found within the adult education system. The first BFI Summer School was set up in 1935 as an adjunct of the Educational Hand Work Association and held over five late summer days in Scarborough. These early courses held during the 1930s were certainly the first of their kind in the country and were reflective of the BFI's approach to film in viewing it as an artisanal craft to be learned and perfected through classes and close instruction. Practical guidance was offered on film projection where students would be allowed to 'manipulate the projector' and perform technical operations in order to fully realise the potential of their own projectors at school level. A number of lectures were also offered, including 'The Film in Education' and 'The Film in National Life' by Reverend F. Heming Vaughan of the Merseyside Film Institute Society. The summer schools continued throughout the following decades, with visits to film studios and lectures on national contributions – primarily British, American, French German, Italian and Japanese cinema – added to the curriculum.

By the time of Paddy Whannel's appointment in 1957, the summer schools had turned into two-week affairs, and by the middle of the following decade, Whannel's influence had fully taken over: students were offered lectures on topics ranging from 'Jazz on Film', the films of Robert Bresson to the 'Vision of John Ford.' Each day at the school commenced with 'illustrated' lectures, followed by afternoons of discussions, before an evening consisting of a full film screening or a lecture. In 1964, one of these lectures was the aforementioned 'The Actor: The Actress', by Peter Sellars and Britt Eklund, then hot property in Hollywood. That year's school also promised to discuss 'what is really new about the recent work of Resnais and Godard? How creative can film makers like John Ford and Howard Hawks be while still remaining inside the popular formula? Do we approach the "art film" in critical terms and the "popular film" in sociological terms?' It is clear that the summer schools provided the clearest exposition of the commitment to ideas, and hospitable to critical thinking espoused in Hall and Whannel's proposals in *The Popular Arts*, published that same year. From an institutional level, the summer schools offered a means for the BFI Education Department staff to test run their own interests and pursuits in film, and culture in general, in front of a ready-made audience. Moreover, the BFI Summer Schools were, by all accounts, tremendously enjoyable – maybe even raucous – affairs which provided an equilibrium between the intensity of the lectures and screenings and the altogether different intensity emerging from the late nights socialising.

Colin MacArthur, an attendee of the 1962 summer school in St. Andrews and who later joined the BFI in 1968, says:

> When I first went there, the Summer Schools featured Paddy Whannel, Jim Kitses, Stanley Reed, Peter Harcourt and Alan Lovell as well. I taught there each year once I joined the BFI, and it was held in places like St. Andrews in Scotland, down in Eastbourne on the south coast, and over to Ormskirk in Lancashire. I remember the disco at one particular Summer School where they went in for flashing lights, psychedelics, strobes, and a screening of The Covered Wagon. I remember one particular summer school on the Western, and they were showing one half of the film on the roof and the other half on the wall! I remember Peter [Wollen] becoming utterly entranced by the whole experience. The summer schools were very welcoming places and never fractious on any level. They were fantastic learning experiences.

Earlier iterations of the summer schools also required students to make a film whereby film-making equipment was supplied by the BFI, and the students' films were shown on the final night. This was discarded by 1964 when the focus of the school was entirely directed towards 'critical appreciation'. This movement from the practical to the critical highlights a notable feature of the summer schools in that they were now positioned to build a cadre of film teachers across Britain. The far-sightedness of the Education Department in hosting the schools across the breadth of the country also meant that distance of geography from London's more active network for film educators was less of a burden. They were also transnational: by the late 1950s, attendees were arriving from not just Britain, but throughout Europe and, on occasion, the United States and Japan. The summer schools allowed for the social life of ideas to blossom within their structure and, after the department's restructuring in 1965 – both financial and intellectual – the focus of the schools turned to contemporary debates in theory.

The programmes for the BFI Summer Schools are very compelling publications in their own right. They provide a map of contemporary interests in film at the BFI at any one time and a very clear break occurs in the schools: the celebrity talks had been entirely supplanted by a range of new approaches including Peter Wollen's syntagmatic analysis of the Western through the prism of Claude Lévi-Strauss's structuralism paradigm and a detailed analysis of the work of John Ford, particularly through the form of auteur-structuralism which Wollen was developing at the time. Further discussions of Budd Boetticher and Nicholas Ray's films followed while the list of students and their work includes future BFI staff, such as MacArthur and Ed Buscombe, but also teachers from across Britain, producers from the BBC, cinema managers and 'housewives' from Norway, and a student from Paris named Dominique Caubet who later became a much-respected linguist. The format of this summer school became the template for the years to follow: the 1968 school was entirely focused upon surrealism; 1969 was devoted to the French New Wave; 1970 was the methods and aims of film criticism; and 1971 concentrated upon the theory and practice of Realism.

'The Summer Schools were just wonderful. They changed people's lives,' reflects Christine Gledhill who worked closely on the Summer Schools programmes.

> One of the things about working at the BFI and being at the Summer Schools is that it was an education for all of us. We were grappling with all this

> new theoretical material. Students and staff were in the same kind of boat, really. [The staff] had the advantage of having longer – we had months of preparation – unlike those who came in as students! But gradually, you take what's useful to you and jettison the authoritative idea that there is only one way to think about things. It also gave me the chance to write. I started to write when I was at the BFI, for example, a two-part essay on about women and film noir – which came out of the very first summer school I taught on. The Summer School opened up such possibilities and BFI Education was amenable to me developing my ideas in this way. Ann Kaplan was at the Film Noir Summer School and produced the Women in Film Noir anthology as a result of it.[1]

The BFI Summer Schools allowed ideas, and arguments were allowed to flourish without the influence of a totalising discourse on film. But these were not the only ways in which the Education Department had increasingly come to resemble a deeply progressive academic space – or in Whannel's terms 'a permanent study laboratory'. We have seen how the increase of resources from the Labour government in 1965 had allowed the BFI Education Department to employ Peter Wollen and Victor Perkins in new roles in publishing and teacher liaison, but also provided space for Wollen to develop his own series of experimental lectures in the basement of the Education Department which were to kickstart the BFI Education Department as a hotbed of theory, debate – and no little antagonism.

## Whannel's team and the BFI education seminars

In 1966, the BFI Education Department moved to new premises at 70 Old Compton Street in central London, sharing offices with SEFT. The premises contained a screening room in the basement and was a two-minute walk from the BFI's primary premises on Dean Street. To the north lay the Soho screening rooms on D'Arblay Street where all the major Hollywood films were pre-screened for industry and press, and even closer was Meard Street which housed the offices of the *New Left Review*. Old Compton Street itself was a rather unsophisticated

[1] Christine Gledhill, personal interview, 31 August 2023. See also the anthology *Woman in Film Noir*, ed. E. Ann Kaplan (London: BFI, 1980). The anthology features essays by Christine Gledhill, Claire Johnston, Sylvia Harvey, Richard Dyer, Pam Cook and Janey Place.

area and one interviewee recalls a gaming arcade run by the Maltese mafia situated opposite the Education Department's office. Soho was still a very lively social environment and, by all accounts, the offices in Old Compton Street were cramped. This combined to create a pressure cooker environment for those working with the department. But the intellectual work also benefitted from the conviviality of Soho. Paddy Whannel and Peter Wollen, along with various members of the department, regularly adjourned to the Admiral Duncan, the long-standing pub in Soho, and home to, variously, mobs in the 1920s and 1930s, to the playwright Dylan Thomas in the 1950s, who lost his only copy of *Under Milk Wood* at the pub in 1953, and has been more commonly known as a gay pub since the 1980s. 'Paddy, personally, was very, very gregarious. He was also a keen beer drinker and darts player,' reflects Laura Mulvey.

> So, all the others [in the department] started playing darts [in the Admiral Duncan] as well. Peter [Wollen] certainly played darts with Paddy. I was a kind of token member of the gang and although it was a very all male, very Hawksian group, I used to join them in the pub. Paddy was very fond of me partly because I knew my Hollywood cinema inside out. I became almost like an honorary member of the gang.[2]

There was a shared outlook amongst the team gathered together by Whannel under the auspices of the BFI Education Department. That they were entirely male is a moot point and it wasn't until the following decade where women played more of an active role in the work undertaken by the department. But the sociability of the groupings, in close proximity to the offices of the *New Left Review*, allows us to trace a web of interactions between the major figures in both institutions, the upshot of which culminated in the BFI Education Seminars, pioneered by Wollen in early 1967. The character of the *New Left Review* had already formed by that point, set by a series of articles by Perry Anderson and Tom Nairn on the nature of British history, and how this informed 'the present crisis'. The journal embarked upon an intemperate debate with the older Socialist tradition, represented by E. P. Thompson whose polemic, 'The Peculiarities of the English' was an outright assault on Anderson and Nairn's theses, criticising them for, among other things, their

[2] Laura Mulvey, personal interview, 6 November 2023.

dismissal of English intelligentsia with Thompson instead pointing towards 'scores of intellectual enclaves, dispersed over England and Scotland'.[3] These theses, effectively, were demonstrating a form of *national nihilism*, a phrase Anderson later located as stemming from an argument he had with Isaac Deutscher with the latter accusing Anderson of 'national nihilism' due to his refusal to engage with politics 'on the ground'. This term was later used by Peter Wollen to describe the *New Left Review* in the 1960s and its irreverent attitude to English culture, and much of this spirit now migrated towards the BFI Education Department.[4]

In January 1967, Whannel wrote an article for *Screen Education* outlining his desire for the department to make a break from the long-standing concept of film appreciation and move towards a more expansive vision of film and education.[5] This came to be known, in Whannel's terms, as 'film culture'. Whannel dismissed film appreciation as 'an outmoded term' and expressed a desire for film to be 'studied in its own right, and increasingly in depth now that there are so many more films worthy studying, and not to be approached as an adjunct to learning about something else'. Whannel signifies an important change in the department's focus, which was to develop the extra-mural courses further and collaborate with universities such as Keele and Warwick, both of which had either been formed or promoted to university status through the enactment of the Robbins Report. Whannel pinpointed these institutions as ideally placed to develop third-level research programmes in film. 'It is hard to see,' insists Whannel, 'how the study of film as an art can be kept out of the new universities, even if it is bound to take time to establish itself.' But before this can happen, he says,

> new educational approaches [need to] draw heavily on its resources – notably on the Library and Information Department. One thing which may not be appreciated is how formidable are the sheerly practical problems of film study – how to get hold of the films to view; how to keep up with film scholarship, when so few places have adequate libraries, and so much of the

3 E. P. Thompson's 'The Peculiarities of the English', *Socialist Register*, 1965.

4 Peter Wollen, *Signs and Meaning in the Cinema*, fifth edition (London: BFI, 2013), p. 527.

5 Paddy Whannel, 'Onward from Film Appreciation', *Screen Education* 37 (January–February 1967): pp. 20–5.

material takes the form of magazine articles published abroad; how to track down facts, as well as opinions'.

Film appreciation was to be comprehensively supplanted by Whannel's vision of the BFI Education Department as a laboratory of ideas and knowledge.

This laboratory was to be fronted by an exciting new initiative. These lectures, known as the BFI Education Department Seminars and designed by Peter Wollen, took place on Thursday evenings in the basement of Old Compton Street, and provided a thrilling and hugely progressive platform for the introduction and discussion of film through the prism of emerging fields across information studies, cybernetics, psychoanalysis, semiotics and structuralism. Figures such as Roland Barthes, Claude Shannon, and Christian Metz were deployed as transnational theoretical reference points across many of these lectures, often spoken about for the very first time in an Anglophone setting. The introduction of theories from France and America reflected the intent on comprehensively revising the likes of F. R. Leavis, Richard Hoggart and Raymond Williams, and the theories underpinning not just the BFI as an institution, but leftist cultural consensus in Britain. Wollen's seminars set about illustrating an exciting new vision for the future of film studies in Britain. Vehement reactions were only to be expected.

Wollen also used *Screen Education* to outline the rubric for the seminars. 'Towards a New Criticism?', an article spread across two pages and illustrated with a still from John Ford's western *Wagon Master* – Ford remained a constant source of inspiration for the Department – takes Whannel's vision and leaps into uncharted terrain for film study.[6] Wollen writes about film in an expansive and strident manner, announcing cinema as 'a new force', and a medium where the existing methods of criticism were critically vacuous due to the lack of engagement with 'sociology, literary criticism, aesthetics and psychology', an oversight which leaves us with a 'primal and innocent blankness' and 'a heuristic void'. To fill this void, Wollen declares that the Education Department's experimental series of film seminars which encompasses 'film critics, film teachers and university teachers and researchers' will investigate 'what kind of interconnections could be made' between the traditional modes

[6] Peter Wollen, 'Towards a New Criticism?' *Screen Education* 41 (September–October 1967): pp. 90–1.

of film criticism incorporating close readings of individual films and directors alongside contemporary work in 'mass media sociology, linguistics and semiology, etc.'.[7]

The seminar space provided a site for the analysis of film through theoretical modes of enquiry. Much of this theory came from the Western Marxism which was being translated and presented a couple of streets away through the work of the *New Left Review*. But whereas that journal was entirely text-driven, these BFI seminars were akin to live research sessions, a place where knowledge and method could intersect in a discursive and fruitful manner. This period of 1967–8 saw other key lectures by Victor Perkins, Peter Harcourt, Andrew Tudor, Alan Lovell and Terry Lovell – the only female figure to speak at the seminars.[8] Each of these lectures were, according to Wollen, indicative of the 'clearest idea of the trend of the seminars [as they succeeded in] confronting different approaches, voicing questions, introducing new concepts and revealing fundamental disagreements' which resulted in a departure from the 'privileged territory of individual taste' and a re-connection of 'judgments' to more 'general, and more abstract, considerations'. Nevertheless, Wollen revealed, 'huge new areas of confusion became apparent without actually being cleared' and he promised a further series of seminars whereby questions would continue to be asked around the distinguishing of 'theory scientific and (singular) from film aesthetics normative and (plural) and [the establishment of a] typology of aesthetic systems'. The answers to these pressing questions, Wollen warned, formed the basis of the 'shimmering and elusive surface of our momentary judgments and remarks'.

The rhetoric employed by Wollen in his article is fascinating, even now. The carefully crafted logic of his argument does not emerge *ex nihilo*; instead,

7 Ibid.

8 A list exists within the BFI papers at the Bill Douglas Centre detailing titles of selected seminars which took place during 1967–9. These titles are as follows: Victor Perkins, 'Film: Technology and Technique'; Alan Lovell, 'The Western'; Peter Harcourt, 'Luis Bunuel'; Peter Wollen 'Eisenstein's Aesthetics'; Tom Nairn, 'Marshall McLuhan'; Fr. Cyril Barrett, 'Film as a Means of Communication'; Alan Lovell, 'Aims of Film Education'; Jim Kitses, 'Author and Genre: Anthony Mann'; Sam Rohdie, 'Totems and Movies'; John Ward, 'Literary Criticism and Cinema Criticism'; Alan Lovell, 'The British Cinema: The Unknown Cinema'; Colin MacArthur, 'Genre and Iconography'; Brian Darling, 'Jean-Luc Godard: Politics and Humanism'; Peter Wollen, 'The Concept of Communication(s): A Draft for Discussion'; Sam Rohdie, 'Style, Rhetoric and Genre'; Gary Herman, 'Words and Pictures'. The Terry Lovell and Andrew Tudor papers are not listed in the BFI list but were spoken about by a number of attendees whom I interviewed. See 'BFI Education Seminars', BFI Education Seminar Papers, Bill Douglas/Peter Jewell Collection, Bill Douglas Centre, University of Exeter.

there is an implicit set of oppositions between modernism, represented by the cinema and emergent disciplines in communication studies and cybernetics, and tradition, represented by 'intellectual isolationism' which implicitly references Perry Anderson and Tom Nairn's contemporary critiques of the national culture in the *New Left Review*. While Wollen writes clearly and free from abstruse theorising or obscure references in this particular article, he does leave the space for the application of ideas and terminology from external disciplines such as linguistics and anthropology to be incorporated through these debates. For Wollen, film studies in Britain was a hopeless and moribund endeavour. He felt that the field was crudely split between Leavisite studies of the work of a select few directors, primarily European, and empirical, mass-media approaches to film through simple-minded psychology. The BFI Education Seminars were his response to this, and his pleas for theory made it clear where he felt the emphasis for film study should now fall.[9]

As we will see, Wollen answered his own plea for a more theoretical engagement with film by commissioning himself to write *Signs and Meaning in the Cinema* in 1968, but his writing at this slightly earlier stage also allows for the opportunity for others to play a role in defining the terms of this new grammar of film. There is a caveat here though – it wasn't just anyone who was allowed to take up this important work. It was limited to those working within specific fields, and primarily men with the requisite confidence to present their work to their peers in the basement of Old Compton Street. It is important to note, too, that the seminars were largely driven through Peter Wollen's initiative, with Paddy Whannel conducting operations behind the scenes. Wollen organised the seminars in a semi-formal fashion, with invitations to speak and attend extended to those within the BFI, and outward towards colleagues within the New Left. These early seminar sessions also produced a 'little book' of their own. *Working Papers on the Cinema: Sociology and Semiology*, edited by Wollen, contained five seminar papers, and it was published in 1969 by the BFI although it appears to have had limited circulation. Certainly, the presentation of the book – a 36-page collection of mimeographed versions of the five selected papers *sans* commentary and devoid of any illustrations – indicates it was not for wider public consumption, but it does demonstrate Wollen's keenness to

9 Peter Wollen, 'Thinking Theory', *Film Comment* 24, no. 4 (July–August 1988): pp. 50–1.

formalise the theoretical discourse undertaken at the seminars. Andrew Tudor was a key member in the construction of the Working Papers booklet although he was operating at that point as a sociologist at the University of Essex along with Terry Lovell. Tudor recalls that Wollen instigated the publication in order to formally introduce new theoretical ideas, specifically from sociology, into the discourse.

> Terry Lovell, Frank West, Paul Filmer and myself all came from sociological backgrounds of course, Terry, Frank and me having known each other in the Leeds sociology department, and we three also being associated (Terry part-time because she had just had a baby) with sociology at Essex in the late 60s. Among those of us in the BFI Seminar set-up who were looking toward France, semiology was the initial interest, with [Roland] Barthes playing an important role and then, of course, Christian Metz. Peter Wollen was [certainly] key here, and I guess the little booklet that we produced in 1969 – *Working Papers on the Cinema: Sociology and Semiology* – was among the first products of that line of thinking. Apart from Peter, the other four of us involved in that were all sociologists, though of somewhat differing persuasion. In a sociological context we had come across Lévi-Strauss by then. Indeed, I recall going to a lecture he gave in London in circa 1966/7 and finding him hugely impressive even though the talk was somewhat impenetrable. Meanwhile, the *New Left Review* folk were absorbing Althusser, with Ben Brewster, in particular becoming evangelical about those theories – and translating, of course. Of course, there were personal links between individuals in both groups. They were no means separate bodies. I expect people just brought other interested parties along for particular topics, and once you started going you got information about what was coming up. They were fun, and sometimes quite combative.[10]

While Brewster would join *Screen* in the 1970s, working as editor throughout the journal's most tumultuous periods, the overlaps between the BFI Education Department Seminars and the *New Left Review* were part of a shared intellectual currency in accord with a desire to import theory from the continent to fill the paucities of Anglophone cultural criticism – a need which, in some respects, aligns Whannel's desire, expressed in the final chapter of *The Popular Arts*, for a study laboratory and Wollen's quest for a more theoretical

10 Andrew Tudor, email interview, 8 October 2019.

approach to cinema. It was in this context that the collision of film studies and theories from the continent occurred. Wollen's reading of theorists was both close and wide, informed earlier by Lucien Goldmann but now by the early-twentieth-century American semiologist Charles Sanders Peirce, Barthes and Metz. But through his own role and freedom within his position at the Education Department, he could commission himself to lecture within the department, educate and advocate – all the while encouraged by Whannel.[11]

With Whannel as the producer and Wollen as the director, the seminars produced a framework and a ferment which went far beyond the local and towards a context where exchange of ideas was encouraged across national and disciplinary boundaries. Wollen was certainly a very eloquent and persuasive advocate of the importance of culture as at least equal to, if not more important than, politics. While he still had a nominal role on the board of the *New Left Review*, his position at the BFI allowed him to break free of the more dogmatic discussions undertaken by the journal at the time. But there was an explosive intellectual charge between the transnational theories being translated and presented in the *New Left Review* and Wollen's vanguardist vision for film. Through this exchange, the BFI Education Seminars emerged as a knowledge-producing laboratory rather like a minuscule university with micro-departments representing the fields of literary criticism, sociology and politics from which a new field could emerge from this interdisciplinary exchange. But not all of the participants in the seminars were impressed with this new form of knowledge. In fact, some were simply baffled as to what Wollen was talking about. Alan Lovell recalled these early seminars with a degree of fond bemusement:

> Clearly the thing which had the biggest impact [on the BFI during this period] was the seminars. I can remember Peter [Wollen] doing the first paper on semiology and nobody had a clue what semiology meant, [and everyone] desperately looking around in dictionaries for the meaning! As

[11] Garry Whannel remembers,

> I would be very surprised if my father was not fairly directly involved [with the seminars] although Peter may well have programmed them. One of my father's skills was [being] so good at employing people and encouraging them – so I would imagine the seminar series had his support and active engagement. I remember [that time] as a 17-year-old, him trying to explain some of the basic principles of semiotic analysis to me! (Garry Whannel, personal interview, 5 May 2020)

> for the seminars [themselves], someone would present a paper, they were conventional in that respect, pretty informal, discussion, we might go the pub afterwards and continue the conversation. Barthes was very important; Louis Althusser was also important, but he came later. Those seminars were pretty open, and a number of people from *New Left Review* came, like Tom Nairn and Jon Halliday. All the ideas of semiology, psychoanalysis, Marxism came out of those seminars, that's my really vivid impulse.[12]

Wollen was responsible for introducing a staggering array of names and concepts through his own lectures, especially his first Education Seminar lecture, 'Cinema and Semiology: Some Points of Contact'.[13] Scanning the text now for references alone reveals fleeting mention of the following writers and theorists: Ferdinand de Saussure, William Morris, Charles Sanders Peirce, Andre Bazin, Sergei Eisenstein, Christian Metz, Roland Barthes, John Stuart Mill, Louis Hjemslev, Samuel Taylor Coleridge, I. A. Richards, Jan Mukařovský, Jean-Jacques Rousseau, Giambattista Vico, Robert Venturi, Johann Georg Hamann, Karl Marx, Vsevolod Meyerhold, Fritz Lenz, John Garrick, Claude Lévi-Strauss, Richard von Foregger, Pavel Tretyakov, Victor Shklovsky, Louis Althusser, Sigmund Freud, Vilém Mathesius, Jiri Veltrusky, Bela Balázs, Johann Lavater, Axel Olrik, Vladimir Propp, Alan Dundes, Umberto Eco, Kenneth L. Pike, Roman Jakobson, Henry Nash Smith, Wilhelm Dilthey, Ernst Cassirer, Immanuel Kant, Georg Simmel, Heinrich Wölfflin, Alois Riegl, Andrew Sarris and Étienne Balibar. No first names were given as part of the lecture and one can only assume that the majority of these figures were unknown to the audience; perhaps only Coleridge, Freud and Marx were names in the intellectual ether, but the others, ranging from fields such as the Prague School of Linguistics and German neo-Kantianism must surely have, as Alan Lovell suggests, been quite puzzling.

This display of intellectual erudition also signifies how the Education Department seminars read now rather like very masculine, gladiatorial affairs where the male speaker would address an audience of Education Department

[12] John Gibbs, 'Interviews: Ian Cameron, V.F. Perkins, Charles Barr, Alan Lovell', *Movie: A Journal of Film Criticism* 8 (2019): pp. 38–71, http://centaur.reading.ac.uk/84433/, accessed 1 May 2020.

[13] Peter Wollen, 'Cinema and Semiology: Some Points of Contact', in *Readings and Writings: Semiotic Counter-Strategies* (London: New Left Books, 1982), p. 17. This essay was originally a BFI Education Seminar paper, to which we will return in the following chapter. It was also published in *Form*, 7, March 1968, edited by Stephen Bann.

staff and reference predominantly male writers and theorists. There was unquestionably a performative element to these seminars; they performed a theoretical education but one steeped in hierarchical and assumed knowledge. The seminars exist as a precursor, but also contrast to the more collaborative role of reading groups which were beginning to play a hugely significant role within the women's movement and to which we will soon return. Occasionally, speakers came from outside the immediate milieu of the BFI; an Irish Jesuit priest, Fr. Cyril Barrett, one of the founding members of the philosophy department at Warwick, spoke about the possibilities of film as a means of communication, referencing Lenin, Leni Riefenstahl and Béla Balázs; Tom Nairn, the Scottish historian and *New Left Review* writer, also spoke about communications through the prism of Marshall McLuhan's work, quoting Roland Barthes's *Elements of Semiology* which had just been published in English for the first time by the publisher Jonathan Cape. Reflecting on the seminars in 2000, Wollen remarked that

> The purpose of the Education Department in the BFI was to launch film education in English schools and universities as a serious subject, alongside the other arts. Painting, literature, music – it was taken for granted that they would be part of the curriculum. So, one of the basic goals of the Education Department was to support anyone who wanted to teach film in schools or universities. And one way to support them was by publishing books which they could use in class. So that was the context in which *Signs & Meaning in the Cinema* was written. There was also a French influence because already the journal *Communications* had been launched in France, where it introduced the ideas of semiology and structuralism.[14]

Furthermore, many of the talks delivered at the Education Seminars were made available for free for teachers to use at their own discretion. And while it is near impossible to reconstruct the take-up of these seminars amongst film teachers at the time, their consistent availability across libraries in the UK, United States, Australia and further afield suggest their dissemination was widespread. But film needed more than lectures and photocopies to become a legitimate discipline for study in schools in universities. There needed to be publications as one cannot teach a subject on which there is minimal

[14] Serge Guilbaut and Scott Watson, 'From an Interview with Peter Wollen', http://www.belkin.ubc.ca/_archived/lastcall/current/page1.html, accessed 4 May 2020.

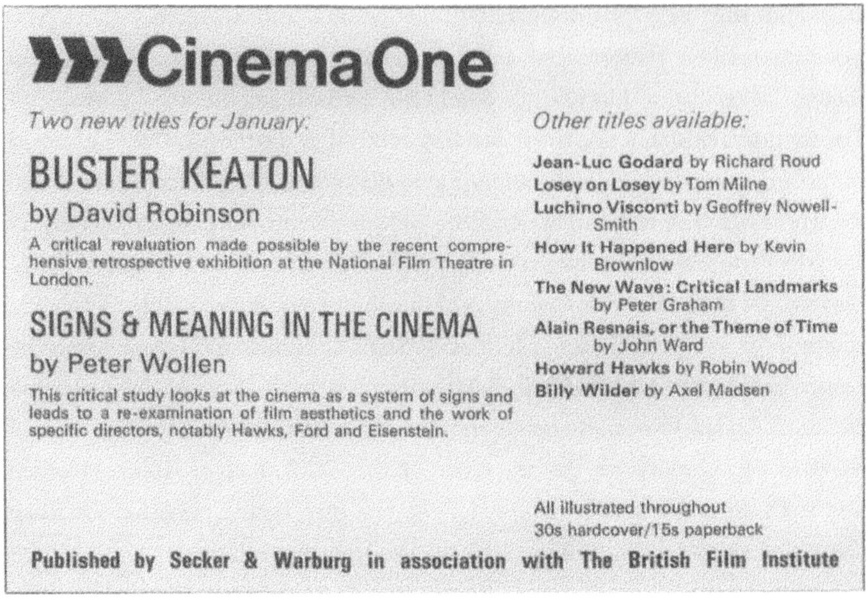


**Figure 10** Cinema One pamphlet, the publishing arm at the BFI.

scholarship. Wollen was aware that there should be 'books which describe the history of what it is, and there should be books that are monographs, and there should be books that approach the subject seriously and more theoretically [than any existing publications]'.

## The Cinema One series

In 1964, the French journal *Communications* published an issue which was a decisive text in shaping and sharpening Peter Wollen's thinking.[15] The issue published both Roland Barthes's 'Éléments de sémiologie' essay and Christian Metz's 'Le cinéma: langue ou langage?' for the first time and was a foundational text in linking semiology and structuralism with film language for the very first time. The Cinema One series, which was the development of a new publishing arm at the BFI devoted to contemporary studies of film, was inspired by *Communications*, and would prove to be one of the

[15] *Communications* 4 (1964): pp. 52–90.

most exciting and contentious initiatives undertaken by the BFI Education Department. Cinema One was an external collaboration between the BFI and Thames and Hudson and an internal collaboration between the BFI Education Department and *Sight and Sound* magazine. In the latter case, it proved to be deeply competitive and costly to both sides. The concept was inaugurated by Whannel and Wollen who proposed a 'program of theoretical film books' – a decision which alerted *Sight and Sound* magazine because it had ceased to publish its own books since the mid-1960s. The two factions embarked upon an uneasy collaboration in order to develop Cinema One as a joint series of publications with books commissioned and edited by a representative of each department. Peter Wollen had primary responsibility for commissioning from the BFI Education Department while Penelope Houston and Tom Milne, editor and deputy editor of *Sight and Sound*, respectively, had responsibility for commissioning writers from their wing of the BFI. The tagline for the series was 'a serious and discriminating venture bringing good critical writing on the cinema to a wide audience'. Each volume was attractively packaged and priced, featuring more than eighty illustrations; while the paperback version sold for 15s, the clothbound sold for 30s. As Wollen points out, this was a very good situation for the publishers as they managed to collate 'a whole range of books, not just a series represented by *Sight and Sound* writing. Many of [the BFI Education Department's] volumes were not only quite different from the *Sight and Sound* tradition but even consciously antagonistic to it.'[16] This antagonism is important: as we will see, *Sight and Sound*'s and the BFI governors' were becoming concerned at the Education Department's extracurricular activities.[17]

In Wollen's view, *Sight and Sound* was 'anti-auteur, anti-experimental and anti-theoretical, yet [the magazine] completely dominated British film

16 Peter Wollen, 'Structuralism Implies a Certain Kind of Mmethodology…', interview with Gerald Peary and Stuart Kaminsky, *Film Heritage* 9, no. 4 (Fall 1974): p. 23. I am grateful to Nicolas Helm-Grovas for providing me with a scan of this article.

17 'I had a big fight with Penelope Houston at this time over the content of my book Underworld USA, she wanting it to be solely about genre rather than, as it is, genre/auteur. In retrospect, she may have been right. I had come into *Sight and Sound* by way of [deputy editor] Tom Milne. He was more relaxed and less disdainful about popular culture than Penelope. She just couldn't understand why [the Education Department were] all getting interested in directors like Sam Fuller. Although there was an overlap; she wrote, or Sight and Sound may have written about Nicholas Ray [whom we were also interested in]. There were also hostile pieces written about auteurism in Sight and Sound and Peter had written that scathing review in New Left Review of Penelope's book on

criticism'.[18] The network of influence within which the magazine operated was also troubling to Wollen, who dismissed their film critics as 'also the people who wrote for the national daily and weekly newspapers and magazines. They all knew each other and provided a training ground for young writers to fill the same mould.'[19] A very clear opposition emerges here: *Sight and Sound* were the gatekeepers, representing tradition and a regressive approach to cinema, meaning 'intelligent, cultivated people who shared an ability to "write well", albeit in a very subjective, impressionistic style, and who regarded the cinema as an important part of "culture" … young dissident critics had no choice but to polarize against it'. The BFI Education Department were these dissidents. They saw themselves as the vanguard and this polarisation was reflected in the split between the Cinema One publications. The series published books on Jean-Luc Godard by Richard Roud, Billy Wilder by Axel Madsen and Buster Keaton by David Robinson, each of which represented a traditional approach to film criticism. But Wollen's commissions, particularly his own *Signs and Meaning in the Cinema*, along with Geoffrey Nowell-Smith's *Visconti* and Jim Kitses's *Horizons West* demonstrated, in differing ways, a startling new theoretical approach, informed by readings of structuralism and semiotics.

These three publications were a natural development from the BFI Education Seminars and much of the theoretical material had already been tested through the format of the seminar. Wollen's use of his own pool of resources is arguably similar to the *Sight & Sound* cadre he was so roundly dismissive of in that his commissioned writers shared an ability to engage with structuralism and semiotics and their opinions were shaped through the Education Seminars, just as Wollen derided the *Sight & Sound* writers for having their own ideas shaped by the film festival circuit. Nevertheless, the theoretical influence on the Education Department at this point was immense. Wollen insisted that

contemporary cinema. She had a fractious relationship with other people broadly on the left at that time, like Boleslaw Sulik, a Polish guy who lived in London and was quite close to the BFI Education Department and that was cemented by the big interest all of us had in Polish cinema at the time. Bolek was connected with some other journals as well and he had written critically about Sight and Sound. I remember discussing this with him and he said Penelope never answered his criticisms in writing, but what she did do was cross to the other side of the street whenever she saw Boleslaw coming towards her!' (Colin MacArthur, personal interview, 1 March 2023)

18 Wollen, 'Structuralism Implies …', p. 24–5. Wollen's criticisms of *Sight and Sound* mirror the earlier criticisms, within the BFI Education Department, of the F. R. Leavis approach to culture, one which is hierarchical and deferential to a pre-defined canon.

19 Ibid.

the published books have a 'theoretical point' and refused for any account of a director to be written in chronological order; instead, they were to be constructed synchronically, demonstrating the structure of a director's work rather than his career. The introduction to Geoffrey Nowell-Smith's book on Visconti laid out this structuralist approach in relatively simple terms:

> the purpose of criticism becomes therefore to uncover behind the superficial contrasts of subject and treatment a structural hard core of basic and often recondite motifs. The pattern formed by these motifs, which may be stylistic or thematic, is what gives an author's work its particular structure, both defining it internally and distinguishing one body of work from another.

Peter Wollen's own *Signs and Meaning in the Cinema* remains the exemplar of the work being undertaken by the BFI Education Department at this time. Published through the Cinema One series in 1969, it remains a hugely influential triptych of essays, demonstrating film, in theory, in remarkably lucid terms. Reflecting on the work some fourteen years later, Wollen recalled writing the book in 1968 when 'structuralism seemed to be an exciting way of going even further with the re-evaluation of popular art' and highlighting 'Lévi-Strauss's analysis of myth' and 'Barthes's semiotic approach in *Mythologies* to popular culture itself' as critiques of popular culture which swerved any form of patronisation. In 1997, Wollen provided a more direct connection between the writing of his seminal book and contemporary political uprising.

> I wrote *Signs and Meaning in the Cinema* in the month of May 1968. As fortune decreed, this has become an emblematic date. May 1968 – it seemed like the beginning of a new epoch. *Signs and Meaning* is full of the same sense of a beginning – a new approach to film studies, a new intellectual seriousness, new theoretical developments, the promise of a new cinema, even the foundation of a new academic discipline.[20]

*Signs and Meaning in the Cinema* was to become emblematic of the BFI Education Department's position as 'intellectual activists'. The book is, as Wollen later pointed out, 'positively heroic in its optimism'. Wollen was not working in a university at the time, viewed himself as more intellectual

[20] Peter Wollen, 'Lee Russell Interviews Peter Wollen', in *Signs and Meaning in the Cinema* (London: BFI, 1997), pp. 211–48.

than academic and was not positioning his writing on film for a university readership because, outside of the BFI's extra-mural courses, none existed. Furthermore, Wollen was working in a period of great intellectual ferment as the wave of nouvelle vague films continued to arrive from France, in tandem with issues of *Cahiers du cinema*. This combination allowed for a re-imagining of Hollywood through the work of relatively obscure directors, readings of continental theory, especially semiotics and structuralism.

*Signs and Meaning in the Cinema* contains three chapters: one on Sergei Eisenstein, another on the auteur theory and a final forward-looking chapter on the semiology of the cinema. Most of this work had been introduced in earlier forms at the Education Department seminars over the course of 1967–8. And just as Paddy Whannel and Stuart Hall's *The Popular Arts* was a *new left* project, *Signs and Meaning in the Cinema* is very much a *new new left* project. Wollen situates the 'haphazard' development of the auteur theory within Anglo-American criticism which has resulted in 'flagrant misunderstandings' amid an ignorance which was 'compounded by a vein of hostility to foreign ideas'. This streak of nihilism is not dissimilar to Perry Anderson's essay 'Components of the National Culture', published in the *new Left Review* in 1968, and both Wollen and Anderson situate Britain as an intellectual backwater, and France as the vanguard of ideas.[21] *Signs and Meaning in the Cinema*'s gaze was firmly directed away from Britain and towards contemporary Europe. Wollen is openly critical of how the auteur theory arrived in Britain 'rather haphazardly' and could be 'interpreted and applied on rather different broad lines', a development which he insists resulted in 'flagrant misunderstandings' within Anglo-American criticism amid an ignorance which was 'compounded by a vein of hostility to foreign ideas'. The work of *Cahiers du Cinéma* in developing the *politique des auteurs* is presented as the counterpoint to the paucity of theory and ideas in Anglophone culture which is depicted as weakly limping behind, unable to keep pace with the sheer pace and methodological superiority of its cross-channel counterparts. Wollen lauds the auteur theory as it allowed for the 're-evaluation of second, Hollywood careers of [European directors]' while

21 Perry Anderson, 'Components of the National Culture', *New Left Review*, 1, no. 50 (July–August 1968): pp. 3–27.

offering a sceptical approach to the 'American director whose salvation has been exile to Europe'. The movement of ideas and value judgements is key here; the auteur theory reverses the trend whereby 'American Renoir was contrasted unfavourably with French Renoir, American Fritz Lang with German Fritz Lang' and the theory is most effective when critiquing movement from a Francophone or Germanophone culture to an Anglophone culture, mirroring the movements of auteur theory and structuralism from France to Britain and America. 'In effect,' reflected Wollen, 'I felt that British culture was stifling, from top to bottom, across classes and my conclusion was that it needed input from abroad to break up its provincialism and insularity. Hence, my interest in Hollywood cinema and French theory came from the same root. It was a kind of pincer movement – low art from across the ocean, high theory from across the Channel.'[22] In linking structuralism with film, Wollen explicitly mentions Roland Barthes's *On Racine* as an essential text, suggesting, in relation to the Westerns of Howard Hawks, that the film critic can 'construct a *homo hawksianus*' in a similar fashion to Barthes's creation of 'a species of homo racinianus'. This sentence is symptomatic of Wollen's quest to overlap an existing field, that of film study, with a methodology purloined from an entirely different field, that of emergent French theory. But Wollen's work also serves to critically undermine a stable position: that of the BFI and *Sight and Sound's* broader work within film criticism. Wollen asserts an entirely new critical vocabulary to think and speak about film – one which was to be taken to theoretical extremes in *Screen* journal throughout the following decade.

Despite the heavy theorizing and Wollen's occasionally breathless approach to listing theorists and concepts, *Signs and Meaning in the Cinema* is not an especially difficult read. It was to prove particularly useful in a pedagogical setting in that Wollen clearly laid out the terms of how structuralism could be used to discuss the oeuvre of a director's work.[23] It was also way ahead of its time. There was simply no comparable book in Anglophone culture which engaged with semiotic theory, structuralism and contemporary film. Wollen was a pioneer. 'Peter Wollen's readings of the auteur and auteur theory were

22 Peter Wollen, 'Lee Russell Interviews Peter Wollen', p. 227.

23 'I found he posed issues in terms of structural oppositions very valuable, pedagogically very useful. I still use them', says Colin MacArthur, personal interview, 1 March 2023.

crucial and [provoked] such interesting debate and discussion,' says Griselda Pollock. 'I'm a witness for the people who were taught by [BFI Education and SEFT staff], and were enabled by this set of people, who formed the high table of this alternative, out-of-institutional education.'[24]

*Signs and Meaning in the Cinema* quickly acquired the resonance of an important text. It is still one of the most commercially successful books ever published by the BFI, and at the time of writing, it is in print in its fifth edition. Within a few years of publication, it was cited by Charles Eckert as being 'after *Film Form* and *What Is Cinema?*, the most widely read work on film theory among present-day film students'. It influenced the work undertaken in film and visual culture departments across Britain and America, as attested by Griselda Pollock. Almost forty years later, film critic Nick Roddick remarked that 'if there is one book to rule them all, it is Peter Wollen's *Signs and Meaning in the Cinema*. The revised and enlarged edition of 1972 is the most concise, lucid, and inspiring introduction to thinking about film ever written.' This appeared as part of a poll on the best books ever written about the cinema – in *Sight and Sound* magazine, of all places. On the occasion of Wollen's death in December 2019, the book was hailed by both the *Guardian* and the *New York Times* as a 'classic text' and a 'film bible', respectively, while the BFI's own Twitter feed referred to Wollen as a 'prophet of film theory'. Yet less than a year after the book's publication, the BFI governors were attempting to force Wollen – and Whannel – out of their positions for being intellectuals and publishing intellectual work at the institution.

It is easy to forget that *Signs and Meaning in the Cinema* was intended as a guidebook for film educators in Britain. Wollen, in his original conclusion, states that he hopes he has 'done something to encourage further study of the cinema, at least by suggesting possible points of departure or stimulating disagreement ... implicit cross-references make themselves felt, which point towards new areas, new zones of study'. These new zones were also influential on Jim Kitses's *Horizons West*, which also appeared under the Cinema One imprint in 1969 and offered a full-length study of three directors – Budd Boetticher, Anthony Mann, Sam Peckinpah – through the prism of auteur-structuralism. Kitses, who was also writing under the influence of Henry Nash

[24] Griselda Pollock, personal interview, 16 January 2023.

Smith's *Virgin Land* which traced the myths and symbols of the historical Westward movement, constructs a structuralist grid to map out the repeated motifs which underpin the Western, a method he describes as 'an ambiguous cluster of meanings and attitudes that provide the traditional thematic structure of the genre'.[25]

These Cinema One publications fostered the work of the Education Seminars and disseminated the ideas far beyond the confines of the basement room in Old Compton Street. But it was the work of the Education Seminars and Cinema One publications which demonstrated both the intellectual reach of the BFI Education Department and its ability to call in people and ideas from the worlds of Marxism, analytical philosophy and film criticism, while also being the initiatives most vulnerable to criticism from both above and outside the institution. It is important to note that the theories expounded upon by Wollen were not intended as a single doctrine which was to be taken as gospel by attendees. Instead, the seminars and publications encouraged and fostered debate and interpretation, and generated scenarios where new forms of criticism could be personally introduced and discussed. There is also a strong sense of collaboration between the BFI education staff even if their positions were occasionally perplexing to one another. Wollen was able to operate with the support and encouragement of Paddy Whannel but also colleagues such as Jim Kitses and Geoffrey Nowell-Smith. But this period of the Education Department's work also represents a sort of intellectual fervour whereby those working for the Department are intoxicated through feverishly reading, interpreting and sharing a whole range of new concepts with which to read and understand film. A remarkable fluidity of movement emerges from simply reading about Wollen, and his cohorts work in connecting and reconnecting an array of theorists and theories to the film horizon until they find one which is most effective in the given moment. Within the rhetoric of the seminars and publications, we witness a form of articulacy emerging around film as a genuine site for study, a vivid and exciting alternative to existing modes of film appreciation, and one which operates in a network of movement, translation and application – and very much alive to the intellectual currents of the contemporary moment.

25 Jim Kitses, *Horizons West* (London: BFI, 1969). See also Henry Nash Smith, *Virgin Land: The American West as Symbol and Myth* (Cambridge, MA: Harvard University Press, 1950).

## Cracks in the edifice

From the mid-1960s onwards, the BFI Education Department had undergone a remarkable transformation. The level of intellectual leadership provided by Whannel was remarkable and much of his vision for the radical overhaul of the Education Department had come to fruition. Moreover, he had assembled a crack team of intellectual activists and agitators and provided them with the tools to carry out their work without undue pressure. Whannel was an enthusiast and an instigator with a particular skill in helping people move forward with their projects. He allowed those around him great space; his relaxed and congenial manner belied a devotion to administration and intellectual seriousness.[26]

But the BFI Board of Governors were increasingly suspicious of Whannel. They were particularly concerned with the type of work he was encouraging under the auspices of an Education Department. They had become wary of the Education Department's work and their apparent 'left-wing' politics – as MacArthur recalls.[27] In late 1968, the Board upbraided Whannel and demanded he provide a full account of the Education Department's activities. Whannel was forced to quickly present both a response and a rationale to senior staff. On 4 November 1968, Whannel met the Board and provided a clear statement of his positioning, and that of the department. He started his plea with a reference to F. R. Leavis, hailing him as the 'key figure in this tradition [of culture and society]' before insisting that within the Leavisite influence, a 'serious engagement with film is impossible' and reiterating the need to engage with funding for potential Research Fellowships which would be operated in tandem with a university department. Whannel further noted

26 'Paddy was such a great enthusiast,' says Ed Buscombe in a personal interview.

> He was a great instigator, good at helping people forward with their projects and so on. He was altogether an inspiration. Peter Wollen never spoke of him except with adulation. On a personal level, he was very important to a lot of people. He stopped writing by the time [Cinema One] came along and saw himself more as an administrator and enthusiast. And someone who could help others to push ahead and so on (Ed Buscombe, personal interview, 22 March 2023).

'Paddy allowed you great space', confirms Colin MacArthur, 'So relaxed and congenial yet serious. Paddy was warm to everyone; he even had a dartboard in his office! He was a superb administrator. You know, at one point I moved into management at the BFI in the Film Availability Service and he was my intellectual mentor when I was trying to formulate policy.'

27 Colin MacArthur, personal interview, 1 March 2023.

that members of the Education staff were already 'engaged in research into aesthetic and critical problems. To that extent the Department operates like a University Department'. It was this repeated insistence on referring to the department as a university which angered the governors. But Whannel was a far-sighted man with a very clear vision: if film is to become a serious academic subject in Britain, it has got to be studied at university level. Whannel felt that promoting this in schools was a dead end and the key to unlocking film as a distinguished subject was through third-level education. Whannel also knew the university system in Britain was not likely to commence this initiative themselves as the concept of a department solely dedicated to film was completely alien to them. It was around this time whereby Whannel conceived the idea of setting up a scheme by which the BFI would offer two universities to pay a salary of a full-time film studies teacher for three years, on the understanding that at the end of the term, the university took over the salary and made the job permanent. It was a seeding operation, in effect, and progressive in its conception. However, the BFI Board of Governors did not share this enthusiasm. Whannel's presentation during the previous November was not met with agreement, the minutes of the meeting indicating that the governors considered Whannel's report to be 'too prescriptive' and 'limiting in its relationship to the wider aspects of film in education'.[28] Still unhappy with Whannel and the department's work, the Education Department was shifted out of Old Compton Street in January 1969 and assimilated into the primary BFI building at 81 Dean Street – where it now shared a floor with *Sight and Sound*. While Whannel spent the summer of 1969 on sabbatical at Northwestern University in Illinois, the antipathy only increased; in April 1970, the BFI governors elected to undertake a comprehensive review of policy at the entire BFI.

The Education Department's work was also under fire from outside the institution. A hostile article by Eric Rhode appeared in *The Listener*, criticising the department not just for taking American cinema seriously but also for its 'strange theories imported from France' with particular criticism reserved for Peter Wollen's *Signs and Meaning* in *the Cinema*, which was dismissed as

[28] See Terry Bolas, *Screen Education*, p. 183.

merely 'esoteric'.[29] Whannel quickly penned a response to Rhode which was both critical and defensive in tone.

> Such assertions of taste are themselves worthless because there is no arguing with them. In place of that we have tried to offer description and analysis and if this implies worth, it need not imply that we think these are major directors or that their work is perfect. Equally, it seems simply an evasion of the challenge represented by Peter Wollen's book to describe it as esoteric. To take one example, it contains the most systematic and elaborated account of an auteur position published in English and which is a model of clarity.... I cannot see anything useful, far less how any intellectual grist, can come out of such an insular attitude.[30]

Whannel was clearly under immense pressure, and throughout the course of 1970, the BFI Board of Governors subjected the BFI Education Department to a gruelling investigation. Meanwhile, a Members Action Group had been set up separately with the specific intention to overturn the governors. The group wrote a manifesto entitled 'Why We Want to Dismiss the Governors'. The group was largely London-centred and featuring Education Department and *New Left Review*-adjacent names such as Peter Wollen, Jon Halliday, Ben Brewster, Claire Johnston, Victor Perkins and Ian Cameron.[31] But the charge against the BFI was that it was an out-of-touch organisation with an out-of-control focus on the spread of Regional Film Theatres and a subservient attitude to the film industry.[32] At the institute's AGM in December 1970, the

29 Eric Rhode, 'The British Cinema in the Seventies', *The Listener* 82, no. 2107 (14 August 1969): p. 201.

30 Paddy Whannel, 'Letter to Eric Rhode', 1970, Nicky North/Paddy Whannel Files, BFI Archive Box 91.

31 Wollen had already left the BFI at this stage but was soon to be appointed to the editorial board of *Screen*.

32 While it's hard not to detect a certain degree of London-centric snobbery with some of these claims, Colin MacArthur suggests that

> although the Education Department may have benefitted from the Jennie Lee grant-two whole new posts were funded shortly after – my recollection is that the bulk of the money went into the creation of regional film theatres. This was certainly Jenny Lee's priority, although she had quite a reductionist view of what regional film development meant, seeing it primarily as a way of bringing Kultur, in the form of filmed performances of theatrical and musical classics, to the great unwashed. Regional expansion was under the control of John Huntley who presided over an utterly mindless expansion into the regions which provoked the wrath of the more thoughtful among BFI staff and was a central theme in the intra- and extra-BFI critiques of regional policy by, for example, the Education Department and the BFI Members Action Group. (Colin MacArthur, personal interview, 9 January 2024)

report on the BFI Education Department had not yet been submitted, leaving the department, and its staff, in a state of despair. But the AGM saw the defeat of the Members Action Group's groups demands – which were already somewhat of a compromise due to the diverse nature of interests across the group's members – and only minor concessions were made to appease their requests. But worse was to come. On 14 January 1971, after almost a year, Asa Briggs delivered his report on the activities of the Education Department. The report was devastating, especially for Paddy Whannel.[33]

*Report of the Review Committee of Educational Services* is a stark, four-page chastisement of the entire work undertaken by the BFI Education Department under Paddy Whannel's leadership. Limited copies were printed – the copy in my possession states 'Copy 6' – but the report is brutal, and its effect was overwhelming and damning. It provides eight points on contention on the work of the Education Department and includes a series of recommendations to streamline the department's work. The report references Whannel meeting with the Board on two occasions in order to explain the 'range and balance' of the Education Department's work and his 'ideas about future development' before admitting that 'Mr. Whannel has made it clear that he is not in full agreement with all the proposals of this report.' The eight recommendations state that the Education Department should variously stick to

> encouraging and servicing other people and organisations, that there should be a gradual reduction in personal writing and lecturing by staff to free [them] for other duties … that the Education Department should concern itself more than it does at the moment with promoting the diverse uses of film in general education as distinct from the study of the art of the film itself or of film criticism … that the right place for sophisticated individual or group research on the film and their impact in educational situations is not in the Education Department of the BFI but in other educational institutions … that the publications policy of the Education Department should be geared to the needs of users of the Institute's services and should have a strong and explicit practical orientation. Within this context responsibility for Cinema One books at present should pass to the Editorial Department.

33 Previous historians of the era, including Terry Bolas, Geoffrey Nowell-Smith and Christophe Dupin, were unable to track down this elusive document, but I have managed to acquire a copy of the report – presumably the only copy still in existence – from Laura Mulvey. *Report of the Review Committee of Educational Services*, mimeographed report (London: BFI, 1970).

The report effectively concludes that the Education Department should cease to be involved with ideas and should simply respond to the needs of teachers with regard to service and materials. There is also an implicit upbraiding of Whannel for encouraging the theory-focused publications emerging from Cinema One; one can infer that Peter Wollen's *Signs and Meaning in the Cinema* was the primary offender. Whannel had successfully marshalled film out of the cul-de-sac of appreciation but now found himself in a cul-de-sac of his own. The institute were no longer willing to fund his pioneering work in a move later described as an 'almost parodic assertion of English empiricism over "foreign theory" '.[34] Whannel refused to cede his territory and embarked upon negotiations with Stanley Reed, his one-time ally, predecessor as head of the Education Department who was now the BFI director. The talks became so fraught that Ernest Lindgren had to act as intermediary between the two sides. In an internal memo from August 1971, the new BFI chairman, Sir Denis Forman, further outlined the issues the governors had with the Education Department, specifically centring upon the department's desire 'to shape a film culture'. It was this very term, according to Terry Bolas, which was the key to their disgruntlement, 'the term that Whannel had long promoted and his repeated references to it seem to have been conflated in Governors' minds with what his department was up to – of which they were perpetually suspicious.' On 31 August 1971, Paddy Whannel resigned his role as the head of the British Film Institute's Education Department. It was quickly followed by the resignation of his colleagues Alan Lovell, secretaries Jenny Norman, Eileen Brock, Gail Naughton and technical officer Jim Pines, who was later to become a leading film academic specialising in contemporary Black cinema.[35]

Whannel's resignation letter was published in *Screen* and circulated to all staff at the BFI. 'The Report was produced in a hasty and ill-considered fashion,' he stated. 'The Governors, none of whom had any experience in film education, felt able to pronounce on our work on the basis of one three-hour meeting.'[36] But the attitude of the governors, and senior BFI management, was one of dismissal – with a strong sense of anti-intellectualism. 'I will only say',

34 MacArthur, 'Two Steps Forward, One Step Back: Cultural Struggle In the BFI', pp. 112–27.

35 See Jim Pines, *Blacks in the Cinema: The Changing Image* (London: BFI Education, 1971) and Pines, *Blacks in Films* (London: Studio Vista, 1975).

36 Paddy Whannel, 'Open Letter to BFI Staff', *Screen* 12, no. 3 (Autumn 1971): pp. 38–43.

wrote Ernest Lindgren in response, 'that when this letter, in its last sentence, argues that the purpose of the British Film Institute is to "play a central role in creating a film culture" it is going against governors' policy and I believe this to be the crux of the whole dispute … it is not the job of the Institute … to develop and promulgate one particular film culture.'[37] It is not difficult to detect the disingenuousness of Lindgren's response: surely the Institute was developing and promulgating one particular film culture and had done so for many years. And whatever one thinks of film appreciation and the idea of a film canon, the institute's brutal closing of its doors to a fresh impetus was alarming.

Much of the ire from Whannel and his colleagues was directed to the role of Asa Briggs, the chairman of the enquiry into the Education Department's work. Briggs was, in Alan Lovell's terms, the very model of a modern academic through his role as vice-chancellor of the University of Sussex, an active historian who was at the time writing an institutional history of the BBC, and respected cultural critic in print and through television. But it wasn't just the BFI Education Department which was under fire from Briggs and his committee. SEFT, the Society for Education in Film and Television, was also under attack from the BFI governors. Prior to his resignation, Whannel had worked out an agreement which delineated the differing functions of these two institutions. The basis of this agreement was that the BFI Education Department would provide lecture services, advisory services, film materials and summer schools, whereas SEFT would provide an annual conference, a summer school designed for teachers and, most importantly, a journal of film education – this was to be *Screen Education* reconfigured as a new journal simply entitled *Screen*. Within a couple of months, a new chairman, Denis Forman, had taken over at the BFI. He met with the remaining Education Department members, and SEFT, and reconstituted the structure of the BFI. Colin MacArthur, who had become Acting Head of Education after Whannel's education, was moved over to Film Availability Services, and took with him views which were sympathetic to Whannel's initiatives. Nicholas Garnham, who was a member of the BFI Members' Action Group, was appointed as a governor, and not long after, the

[37] See 'Correspondence Connected with the Resignation of Whannel and Others', BFI Archive, Nicky North/Paddy Whannel Files, Box 91.

Education Department – now renamed the Education Department – was able to continue the work undertaken by Whannel in a manner which nobody could have foreseen. But the resignation of Paddy Whannel brought an end to an era of rare and unparalleled innovation at the BFI. It is difficult to imagine a comparable cultural institution in Britain at this time undertaking such radical work across the field of education and communication. The line which stretches from the Butler Education Act of 1944 through the commitments of Adult Education and over to the activities of the Education Department under Whannel brings together otherwise discreet activities under a single structure of pedagogical encouragement and intellectual curiosity. However, the era of film and theory was far from over. In fact, the 1970s was to bring an entirely new configuration of theoretical approaches to the fore at the BFI and especially *Screen* journal.

3

# Film Theory in the 1970s and *Screen* journal

## The London film scene, reading groups and the women's movement

As the 1960s gave way to the 1970s, the travails of the BFI Education Department show us how the site of film had become a deeply contested space. The disputations and conflict at institutional level became proxies for wider conversations about national cinema, the changing role of criticism in mid-century Britain and the role of cultural institutions within the wider landscape. The intellectual work encouraged by Paddy Whannel and his team managed to forge new alliances between Hollywood and continental theory, but it had also provoked a form of sociological antagonism which was to continue in varying forms throughout the following decades. But film, and film discourse, was more widely available than ever by the turn of the decade. For any film enthusiast in London during the 1970s, the city was rich with screenings, independent cinemas, reading groups and forums all dedicated to the radical potential of cinema. Many of these different trends were working with each other in hugely different ways, but as we will see, these trends were able to speak with each other and could provide a positive impact upon the development of cinema as a site for political and personal change. The form of collective which characterised much of the intellectual and theoretical work around film throughout the decade provided massive encouragement for those wishing to work with film on a deeper, more politically and socially engaged level. This impetus was, in part, due to Jennie Lee's encouragement of film on a governmental level, allocating generous resources to the arts. Along with the BFI, art schools were flourishing, and cultural institutions were more than ever able to employ intellectuals, agitating for continental theory, avant-garde film-making, exploring intersections between disciplines and fostering creative energy on a grand scale. The BFI was central to this positive intersection between funding and progress; indeed, the concept of progress was kept largely separate to management concerns. The availability of funding meant there was simply more space for progressive ideas to take hold and result in dissemination of ideas and, ultimately, production of new work. This distribution of ideas, of funding, and of actual films was also critical to developing this invigorating community of film-makers. For emerging film-makers – and indeed many enthusiasts of theory – the only way to experience film was to be able to see the films they were reading about in these journals. But film had developed its own form of cultural capital unique to the late 1960s and early 1970s. Film was mobilised for political purposes, and an intoxicating era of screenings, talks, reading groups and publications was ushered forth. Laura Mulvey recalls:

> By the early 1970s, consciousness of cinema had begun to change in the UK. And Pam and Andi Engel set up Politkino primarily to bring Jean-Marie Straub and Danièle Huillet's films into UK distribution. Godard was very important for Peter [Wollen] around this time. So, these new distributors really contributed to the changes in film culture … that is, if distributors hadn't made experimental films available, we wouldn't have seen them.[1]

An important moment was the tour of avant-garde film from America, organised by P. Adams Sitney in April 1968.[2] The tour featured works by Stan Brakhage, Ken Jacobs, Peter Kubelka, Jonas Mekas, Harry Smith, Andy Warhol and many more, and took in visits to twelve universities alongside a week of programmes at the NFT. While Sitney was sceptical about the immediate reception of the films in a British context, the tour was a significant catalyst for discussion of new forms of film, and prompted a major interest in underground, avant-garde film through the work undertaken by the New Oxford Cinema Club and especially the critical and activist work of Peter Sainsbury and Simon Field who were then working at the University of Essex. Mulvey continues:

> I think this is true: P. Adams Sitney left behind his collection of films at the London Film Makers Co-op, which contributed to making the New

1 Laura Mulvey, personal interview, 6 November 2023.
2 See Michael O'Pray, *The British Avant-Garde Film 1926–1995*, pp. 106–7.

American Cinema known in the UK. In 1973, Simon Field and David Curtis organised The International Festival of Independent Avant-Garde, which had a huge impact on me. That's where I first saw films by Yvonne Rainier, Chantal Akerman, Joyce Wieland – all together in this one season at the NFT. I was probably still writing 'Visual Pleasure and Narrative Cinema' then ... while the essay was/is primarily a critique of Hollywood, it also recognised that a new kind of women's cinema was beginning to emerge. Here again one sees the importance of programming, of making films available, in the circulation of new ideas.

Simon was very keen for Chantal Akerman to meet Peter and me. We met her milling around at the NFT. I asked her where was she staying and she said, "I'm staying in a real horrible place, I don't like it at all" so I said, "come stay with Peter and me!" and so, she packed her stuff and moved in with us. One evening [at our house] there was a meeting of the women's liberation group that I belonged to, Chantal asked, "could I sit in?" and I said "of course" and then, as usual [at the end], everyone started packing up soon after 10pm. Chantal was flabbergasted! She said, "why did you stop? It was a really interesting conversation you had going!" and I said "well, they have to get the bus home" she said "What! You actually stopped because getting the bus! We would never have done that in France!" I felt mortified! We were clearly petit bourgeois English people in Chantal's eyes.'[3]

The plethora of intellectual activity in London around film discussion during the 1970s now seems remarkable. Along with the increasing availability of avant-garde films and film-makers, there was an enormous influx of French and German theory being translated and published in Britain, much of it appearing out of sequence with its original publication in French or German. This created a form of theoretical delirium whereby ideas and concepts were being received for the first time in an Anglophone context, but thrillingly disconnected from their original contexts be that Francophone psychoanalysis, cultural anthropology or any other melange of theory and interpretation. It was not possible to study such as Louis Althusser, Jacques Lacan, Walter Benjamin or Michel Foucault at a university level – even the use of Marx and Freud were still controversial figures at an institutional level – and alternative spaces had to emerge in order to unpack this thrilling, but often quite difficult, material.

3 Laura Mulvey, personal interview, 6 November 2023.

As we saw in the previous chapter, Peter Wollen's BFI Education Seminars provided one method of disseminating such material, but more of this theoretical material was now available for consumption – often at a reasonable price. But the lecture format was rather hierarchical, and did not always allow for collaborative, or group, interpretations. Instead, it was the development of reading groups which provided a more benevolent manner of reading and unpacking these theories. Reading groups played an unparalleled role in the theoretical education of the generation of socially engaged intellectuals during this period, particular within the women's movement. The History Group, a reading group for women, was founded directly after the influential Oxford Women's Conference in early 1970. Its founders, Rosalind Delmar and Juliet Mitchell, quickly joined by Mary Kelly, an American artist who spent time on the *Screen* board in the late 1970s, and Laura Mulvey. The group emerged from the Women's Liberation Workshop which was, according to Rosalind Delmar, a 'loose network of mainly all-women groups' with the History Group its first official study and reading outreach collective.[4] Much of this impetus stemmed from work undertaken by Juliet Mitchell, whose essay 'Women: The Longest Revolution' was published in the *New Left Review* in late 1966.

> We didn't initially call [the movement] feminism in England. We called it women's liberation and like Simone de Beauvoir, we had been very critical of what had happened with first-wave feminism and with Christabel Pankhurst – we were fighting shy of calling it feminist. But by then, it was quite a strong movement, so I went [to America] to talk with Stokely Carmichael when he said the place for women in the movement was prone and I argued with him – not that he took any notice of me whatsoever! And I went to look at Watts [the suburb of Los Angeles which erupted in 1965 over racist practices by the LAPD] – America was pretty important to me at that point and that's where I found all this protest against Freud and psychoanalysis, and I got interested in that while I was in America. Because it wasn't a big theme [in Britain].[5]

Mitchell's reading group was hugely formative for women who wanted to understand theory and knew they could achieve this by reading it as a group

[4] See 'On the Passage of a Few People through a Rather Brief Period of Time' for a rich account of this era. https://www.tate.org.uk/documents/999/on_the_passage_of_a_few_people_through_a_rather_brief_period_of_time.pdf, accessed 10 June 2024. The quote from Rosalind Delmar is on page 4.

[5] Juliet Mitchell, personal interview, 28 January 2023.

rather than working all by oneself. More and more reading groups started to emerge across London, some dedicated to reading Marx's *Capital*, other worked on Lacan and Foucault. By default, reading groups offered a structure and a deadline and an overwhelming sense of unified collaboration, working towards a form of mutual understanding. Mandy Merck, who was to edit *Screen* journal throughout the 1980s, recalls the gravity of these reading groups.

> How did [all of these] reading groups start? We formed them. The first reading group that I can recall read Juliet Mitchell's *Psychoanalysis and Feminism*. My girlfriend was a PhD student in history. We both wanted to understand it better than we could if we just tried reading it by ourselves. And then I joined a [Marx's] *Capital* reading group. And you read a chapter, took notes, and if you didn't understand what Marx means here – [you would ask people to] explain. Part of it was just exposition. Freud was exposition but also application.[6]

The BFI Education Department played a very important role in working with the women's movement and promoting women's cinema.[7] From 1974, Claire Johnston, to whom we will return, taught a course on Women and Cinema as an extra-mural course at the University of London – Paddy Whannel's initiative still remained an integral part of the department's work – and through the BFI Educational Advisory Service, the Women and Film Group made freely available an extensive typescript containing the syllabuses of twelve pioneering courses relating to 'women and film/images of women in the media' with Christine Gledhill and Nicky North, in particular, playing vital roles in collating information relevant to the development of syllabuses connecting the women's movement with the study of film. In providing information about courses, many of which were taught by film scholars including Julia Lesage, Ann Kaplan, Sylvia Harvey and collectives at the University of California and Polytechnic of Central London, along with offering a service to provide film prints relevant to each course, the Education Department continued the crucial work of reading groups in creating spaces for collective work on films about the lives of women – often working-class

6 Mandy Merck, personal interview, 23 October 2023.

7 The department was renamed the Educational Advisory Service in 1971 but returned to Education Department by the end of the decade. I have retained the original title throughout to avoid confusion.

women – through a collaborative engagement with contemporary feminist politics. The integration of production, exhibition, distribution and reading were central to these politics of representation and social organisation and the BFI Education Service provided essential institutional legitimacy and national levels of influence. Merck continues:

> What was brilliant [about that time] is that the barriers between professions were much lower. If you were willing to do the work, nobody challenged your right to do it. Because no one had advanced degrees in post-structuralism or psychoanalysis – they didn't exist. Certainly not in film studies. The best place in London to study film would have been the Polytechnic of Central London. I ended up teaching there. When I got involved in the *Capital* reading group, I got through all of volume one, most of volume two, but I left at volume 3 – the transformation problem – I'm still not sure what the point of it was. Sometimes men were part of these groups – it wasn't a big problem. And psychoanalysis – we started doing reading groups in that. There was a great Freud reading group that had people like Cora Kaplan in it, that I was in for a couple of years, Barbara Taylor was in it, too. I remember we read the Meta-Psychology volume of the Pelican volumes which is a great introduction to key issues. When people talk about reading groups now, I think my entire life has been a reading group![8]

## The pump-priming operation of film into universities

By this point in the mid-1970s, Paddy Whannel had left the country to take up a position as professor of film at Northwestern University in Illinois – one of his students in his very first year was a young film director by the name of James Jarmusch. Peter Wollen had left Education Department as publications officer, replaced by Christopher Williams, and, along with Laura Mulvey and their son, Chad, was soon to join Whannel at Northwestern. After the disruption of the BFI Governor's Report in 1971, the department's role was ostensibly reduced by the new Board of Governors: The department was ordered to simply respond to the needs of film teachers and providing services and materials where necessary.

[8] Mandy Merck, personal interview, 25 October 2023.

Despite the resistance to ideas and innovation which marked the BFI governors' sweeping critique of the Education Department, those staff members who stayed, along with the influx of new faces, many of whom had been schooled through the summer schools in the previous decade, maintained the commitment to openness. Much of this was quite fiercely resisted by the management at the BFI, but also other departments within the institution who felt the Education Department's work was frivolous. This view was patently ridiculous. But one of Paddy Whannel's most pioneering and important initiatives was about to be revived by the BFI. Despite the progress made by the Education Department in lecturing and publishing in film as a serious site for study, film studies was not yet a fully realised university subject. There were opportunities to study film at the BFI/University of London extra-mural evening courses, and progressive academic spaces such as the aforementioned Polytechnic of Central London were offering courses in film and photography.[9] These evening classes, however, were now to form the basis for a remarkable seeding operation, bringing the study of film into universities across England and Scotland. This was known internally as the 'pump-priming' operation, outlined by Paddy Whannel in his final years as head of the Education Department. The strategy was thus: the BFI would pay the lecturer's salary for the first three years with the expectation that the university would take over the appointment at the end of that trial period. The first post to be created was at Warwick University with Robin Wood as lecturer, set up in October 1973. This was the very first film studies position in a British university which treated film as an autonomous discipline and with a degree course as its ultimate aim. Perhaps ironically, Wood's own background was deeply rooted in English literature and the school of F. R. Leavis – which brought him into regular conflict with some

[9] The artist and theorist Victor Burgin was a lecturer at the Polytechnic at the time. 'I wound up taking a BFI evening class designed by Ben Brewster,' says Burgin,

> which took the form of seminars led alternately by Brewster and Colin MacCabe. The readings were chosen and organised by Brewster, and the seminars began with a presentation, by either the seminar leader or a member of the class, followed by class discussion. That really was an extraordinary foundation course. I had already read Roland Barthes' *Elements of Semiology*, but Brewster's course helped bring me up to speed in structural linguistics to the point I felt confident in introducing Barthesian semiology into my teaching at the Polytechnic of Central London – with the difference, of course, that I was bringing it to the analysis of photographs rather than film. (Victor Burgin, personal interview, 28 February 2023)

members of the BFI Education Department – and his course focused upon the 'potential value of art on a personal level, as enriching, refining, developing, modifying the individual sensibility'. None of the recent developments in film theory appeared to influence Wood's position although *Signs and Meaning in the Cinema* was a key text on his course. The course was successful; within three years, the Board of Arts at the university had unanimously agreed to set up a joint degree in Film and Theatre Studies, to begin in October 1977; an influential film magazine entitled *Framework* was formed by Jenny Norman and Elizabeth Ahearne in 1973 and Warwick became a celebrated centre for film culture with Victor Perkins a long-standing member of the department.[10]

The universities interested in the scheme were all new, red-brick universities and the BFI made sure to have a representative on the interview board for each university appointment. This ensured the jobs went to those who already had some relationship with the film education work being undertaken at the institution.[11] Once Warwick took up the initial option of funding the film studies course themselves, this released the finance for more university positions. Richard Dyer – whose PhD thesis on musicals was externally supervised by Paddy Whannel – took up his position at Keele while Peter Wollen, returned from Northwestern University in Illinois, took up his role at the University of Essex. Wollen's introductory lecture in January 1975 reads strikingly even now.[12] He tantalised students and staff in proposing a one two-year seminar which

[10] 'Paddy basically set up a scheme whereby the BFI would offer universities to pay a salary of a full-time film studies teacher for three years on the understanding that at the end of three years, they took it over and made the job permanent,' says Ed Buscombe now.

> It was a great idea. My job was to run that, which was fascinating, because we invited applications – universities were always hungry for money – so they were lining up to get one of these posts. And so, I would go round to all the universities that approached us and check them out. They would tell me what was going on and what their interest might be in film and so on. And I would come to a conclusion as to what extent they were serious, to what extent we could trust them to take on the post. (Ed Buscombe, personal interview, 22 March 2023)

[11] 'It was quite a responsible position! So, over the course of the next three or four years, we made a number of appointments. They had appointed Richard Dyer to Keele, over the course of the next few years, we started up jobs at East Anglia, and Kent, and Warwick, and Stirling, and they were all new universities. And also, Essex, where Peter Wollen came back to from Northwestern University. All the people who were appointed to these jobs were pretty notable people: Victor Perkins, Thomas Elsasser, Charles Barr and so on. One of the conditions of us giving them money was that I sat on the interview board with a vote, so I could swing the job to people whom I thought were most qualified and would make something of it.' Ibid.

[12] The lecture was recounted by an unknown author in the student newspaper *Ghost Times*, 17 January 1975 (Essex: University of Essex), pp. 1–2.

would reveal 'the whole suppressed experimental film inside Citizen Kane', but also, stressed the need for empirical work in analysing the interrelation between codes in cinema. Wollen quickly established classes in semiotics, narrative structure and de-structure in film, and Soviet cinema. 'Peter was a brilliant teacher and contributed a lot to what they were doing [at the University of Essex]', says Laura Mulvey. 'Nowadays that wouldn't happen. In those days, film studies was so new. Film studies needed people. It was a seller's market.'[13]

Each of the film courses inaugurated under the BFI's tutelage had a theoretical underpinning, whether Leavisite or otherwise, and emerged at a time of rich cultural ferment, when film started to become stabilised as legitimate academic subject. The work of the BFI Education Department as a collective in calling for film to be studied with a critical apparatus was vindicated. The nascent film studies classes became a space whereby theories from linguistics, literature, philosophy and anthropology were allowed to flourish. It became an extraordinarily wide spectrum of tendencies which, at its most progressive, radicalised film as an extension of modernism. 'There was, also, on another level a similarity [between film and] fairy and folk tales,' said Peter Wollen in 2006 while reflecting on his time at Essex.

> [These] were the basis for Roman Jakobson's theoretical writings, which had also influenced Lévi-Strauss ... my first job in a university in England ... goes back to Jakobson and so on – that's why the people in Colchester [Essex] were interested in my approach to the cinema. You had a university with a linguistics department [there] that had people who were well aware of [Vladimir] Propp already because they were Slavic scholars. Suddenly film studies brought into play the ideas of people like Propp and Jakobson. From this you then had the possibility of film being taught in British universities. None of that could have been predicted.

The success of Whannel's initiative was extraordinary. Film studies became a recognised and established part of curriculums across the majority of universities in Britain. At this juncture, in the 1970s, film was also primed to establish itself as a major intellectual discipline. The 'pincer movement', as earlier described by Peter Wollen, of high theory from Europe and Hollywood – and now avant-garde – films from America provided a stimulating current

[13] Laura Mulvey, personal interview, 6 November 2023.

of thought which fed into not just the emergent field film studies but into the humanities at large, creating provocative and often fraught new lines of enquiry. As we have seen, much of this activity, across different networks and scenes, may feel heterogeneous yet a core focus is discernible: the deployment of film and theory and challenges to existing orthodoxies.

## Film in schools

While much of the work being done in and around the BFI Education Department had an outward focus upon third-level study, there was also inspirational work being undertaken in getting film studies out to secondary schools across Britain. While universities were gradually taking on the idea of film studies as a subject, the BFI felt that this wasn't quite enough, especially if film was not studied or examined at second-level schooling. David Lusted recalls:

> Around this time, an opportunity arose to join a consortium of London-based teachers bent on persuading some regional exam boards to offer Film Studies at GCE O and A Level. (The same group of teachers went on to write the syllabuses.) On the strength of that history, I'm sure, I got offered a new post as Regional Education Officer at the BFI. Part of my spiel at the interview was a response to the Education Department's then push for academic appointments in HE to establish film studies as a discipline, constructing degree courses in the subject. I argued that wasn't enough without also building a body of film study teachers in secondary and further education – and not just in London but all over the UK – who would be producing students from the O and A Level courses, many of whom would choose to go on to study at degree level.[14]

Lusted immediately set to work on setting up syllabuses at O Level and later at A Level in film studies across England and Wales. 'That became the first task in my regional brief,' he says,

> to build a network of teachers enabled and committed to teaching film studies in schools and FE. The education system at the time had an elaborate infrastructure of local education authorities (LEAs) with Teacher In-Service

14 David Lusted, personal interview, 31 March 2023.

Education provision. Later, Thatcher administrations destroyed that localised national structure in order to centralise control over the education system. So what BFI Education was able to do then, wouldn't be possible again. But in my time, it enabled contact with groups of teachers through a network of teacher advisors across the country. It meant that the Dept. could set up and run in-service courses for teachers willing to attend in their own time. As a result, at my busiest, I was traveling the country making contacts and setting up courses, all taught by BFI Education staff. I could be in Molde in north Wales on Monday, Peterborough on the Tuesday, Luton on a Wednesday, and so on, meeting enablers and arranging courses. From that initiative, individuals and groups became responsible for their own local initiatives, initially assisted by a little BFI seeding money. In a few years, there were in-service film courses running all around the country, teachers learning from them and then teaching courses for their own students, including the new film courses at O and A Level.

Out of that experience came the idea for teaching materials. The Education Dept. had advisory documents for teachers and film extracts for classroom study, but it lacked teaching materials to aid and guide teachers. Primary school teachers, in particular, weren't really served. There was a practice of schoolchildren attending screenings in film theatres at the time, but teachers had little conceptual language to talk about the films with their kids afterwards, so the screenings tended to stand alone. Some staff in BFI Ed. made slide sets for their own purposes by copying, with permission, film frames. I made slide sets from films like *The Railway Children* for study with primary age groups, accompanied by notes with very simple suggestions for introductions, questions to ask children to stimulate discussion and so on, drawing on skills primary school teachers already had. It took off in some places. A regional film theatre would show a film, I'd talk briefly with the teachers, giving them a slide set to take back to their classrooms. Some would return to talk about what happened, then I'd give them another slide set for another film, and so on, until it became a regular practice. Sometimes it worked well, with teachers forming groups and asking for more, but too often it didn't go down well at all: those teachers just wanted the film experience. But over the years, dozens of teachers around the country were not only taking groups of primary age children to film theatre screenings but also talking about films in their classrooms.[15]

15 Lusted continues,

> Later, during the 1970s, Cary Bazalgette came into the department because she had primary school experience, she knew about the importance of teaching materials. Under her inspiration, cyclostyled advisory documents were augmented by a range of more

Many of these teaching aids and advisory documents survive in the BFI archives in the Bill Douglas Centre at the University of Exeter.[16] They remain remarkable documents, showcasing a depth of intellectual engagement with a vast range of topics: the crime film, the gangster film, censorship, realism, formalism, Bazinian realism, Black cinema, women in film, men in film and homosexuality in film. The study materials offer an uncompromising critical edge with a strong educative accent. The writing is informed and shows a deference to a spectrum of fields including aesthetics, semiotics, ideology, sociology and economics. On reading the materials now, it is clear that they were developed and made available in that collective spirit of film, education and challenging orthodoxies – and while 1970s film theory is often confined to examinations of the work of *Screen* journal, which we will come back to, it is equally important to fasten the structural work undertaken by those at the BFI Education Department in developing film studies as a serious site for study by all those in education. It was not just directed towards an audience au fait with contemporary theoretical developments from across the channel and beyond. The advisory pamphlets and especially the superb library of 16-mm extracts available for film educators to use in their classes were all part of the wider move to have film recognised as its own constituency, distinct from English literature or theatre. There is a durability to this work in that so many of the concepts written about as part of these advisory documents did make their way down into the secondary school system and into our everyday readings of film and media. The service was pioneering in treating students as capable of working with and understanding a radically pluralist range of topics through the prism of film.

professionally produced teaching materials. A slide collection started to grow. Cary was instrumental in all of that – she also widened the take-up of film studies within media education, particularly important for its penetration into the primary sector. Film studies was most active in secondary schools and the FE system, though, where activity continues despite the purges of the humanities by Conservative administrations. Many teachers want to teach about film – even where, as a subject, it can't be taught – at least as part of media studies, and kids are receptive to learning about it. As long as there are committed teachers and kids who want to learn about film, it will be happen. (David Lusted, personal interview, 31 March 2023)

16 For example, David Lusted, ed., *Guide to Film Studies in Secondary and Further Education* (London: BFI Education, 1983) is a remarkable survey of teaching film studies, across Production, Animation, Genre Studies, Industry, Narrative, Politics, Star and Gender Studies. The archive also contains invaluable study documents on Black cinema, queer cinema and the Western, written by Jim Pines, Richard Dyer, Ed Buscombe and many more. See Bill Douglas and Peter Jewell Collection, Bill Douglas Cinema Museum, University of Essex.

## *Screen* journal

The remarkable work undertaken by the BFI Education Department during the 1970s occurred in spite of the continuing opposition to the department's work. But the theories emerging from the Cinema One publications and Peter Wollen's seminars soon found a new outlet in *Screen* journal. *Screen* remains one of the most significant journals in the entire history of film studies. It was within the pages of this publication where the gladiatorial approach of the BFI Education Seminars continued its trajectory. During the period 1971–9, *Screen* was where the grand narratives of Marxism, semiotics and psychoanalysis found a unique place in British critical thought. It resulted in some of the most illuminating, challenging, even onerous, set of analyses on film in the Anglophone world. It was also the journal where Laura Mulvey published her essay 'Visual Pleasure and Narrative Cinema' in 1975, coining the term the 'male gaze', arguably the single most influential feminist polemic for film gender dynamics. *Screen*'s emergence as theoretical powerhouse was directly linked to the BFI Education Department's resignations of 1971. The journal was re-configured as a well-funded site to explore the very same ideas

**Figure 11** *Screen* journal, Autumn 1972.

that the BFI Governors decided would not be explored within the BFI itself. *Screen*, therefore, was operated by SEFT.

*Screen* had been in existence in some form or other since 1952, as a descendant of *The Film Teacher*, a newsletter which was distributed by the Society of Film Teachers, and offered practical advice for aspiring teachers of film and television, before later rebranding as *Screen Education*. But in 1969, just as the BFI Education Department was coming under attack, the journal was relaunched by SEFT under the editorship of Terry Bolas and Kevin Gough-Yates. Almost improbably, as the BFI Education Department was imploding under the weight of the resignations and pressure from the BFI Governors, the journal was revamped yet again under the editorship of a pugnacious young American named Sam Rohdie. The journal received a new modernist design and embarked upon on an exceptional decade of high theory, radical potential and belligerent dispute – all within the name of film, in theory. The new design for *Screen* was created by Gerald Cinamon, a book designer for Penguin who had also worked with New Left Books, an offshoot of the *New Left Review*.[17] Cinamon's cover design for *Screen* was both strident and striking: a single vertical strip bisected the page with the *Screen* letters arranged in a fashion resembling their horizontal motion; to read the title *Screen* one had to read vertically but all of the other information on the cover, including the titles of specific articles, was written at a right angle to the *Screen* title. Immediately, it was clear that this new iteration of *Screen* was not planning on making it easy for its audience.

> I suppose one of the editors noticed my designs for Penguin covers and thought that *Screen* should modernise its covers. I'm sure there was no design brief from the editors [but] clearly, I tried to suggest *film movement*. I think I had lunch with Sam Rohdie in the very early days. He seemed to be 'in charge' of design matters … I don't think I ever met the others, but … every time I phoned there seemed to be arguments going on in the background![18]

17 Cinamon had recently designed *A Fortunate Man* (London: Allen Lane, 1967), a collaboration between writer John Berger and photographer Jean Mohr on the working life of a country doctor in the Forest of Dean.

18 Gerald Cinamon, email interview, 27 September 2020.

Rohdie had arrived in Britain from the United States having spent time in Ghana in between.[19] It was through socialist circles there where he encountered Roger Murray who was on the board of the reconstituted *New Left Review*. Murray introduced Rohdie to Peter Wollen, and other key figures in the New New Left including Jon Halliday and Ben Brewster. On his move to Britain from Ghana, Rohdie secured a teaching position at Sheffield Art College – later Sheffield Hallam University – and lectured on social anthropology and film, deploying positions taken from his readings of *Cahiers du Cinéma* and his own interpretations of both American cinema and the nouvelle vague. Amidst all the upheaval in the BFI Education Department, Rohdie was hired as general secretary of SEFT. With this post came an important engagement: the editorship of *Screen* journal. 'I knew Sam from his work in Sheffield,' said Alan Lovell. 'I also knew his partner Jean McCrindle from the *Universities and Left Review*. I encouraged him to apply for the SEFT job which he did. Sam was the guy who really plunged us right into the middle of French theory. He invited Stephen Heath and Colin MacCabe onto the board [of *Screen*] and then we were right in it!'[20]

Rohdie's influence is overlooked in most contemporary accounts of *Screen* but his influence on the journal's direction during the early part of the 1970s was immense.[21] Rohdie was responsible for giving space to Stephen Heath and Colin MacCabe, female writers such as Claire Johnston, Terry Lovell and Kari Hanet, and he even had the chutzpah to criticise and undermine articles published in *Screen* itself if he disagreed with them. Moreover, Rohdie certainly appeared to have the capacity and confidence to effect

[19] Deane Williams, 'Some Things You Never Learn: An Interview with Sam Rohdie', http://www.screeningthepast.com/issue-28-australian-film-culture-australian-research-council-interviews/some-things-you-never-learn/, accessed 10 June 2024.

[20] Alan Lovell, personal interview, 12 January 2021. Jean McCrindle was a prominent feminist and left-wing activist.

[21] Sam Rohdie died in 2015. Many of his obituaries testify to his difficult character; see, for example, Adrian Martin's account where he describes Rohdie as

> aggressive and provocative inside the classroom, just as he could be more than a little sociopathic and monstrous outside it; he was impatient with having to be 'the teacher' (let alone an administrator). This seems to have remained his teaching mode, more or less, to the end of his life (he was about to retire from the game in May 2015 – a cycle of financial gambles, bad investments and disasters throughout his life had prevented him from leaving any earlier).

Adrian Martin, 'Sam Rohdie', http://www.filmcritic.com.au/essays/rohdie.html, accessed 10 August 2020.

considerable change; his time at the helm of the journal is marked by the dominant critical and formal ideologies of *Screen*, SEFT and, by proxy, BFI Education, rotating rapidly in the direction of theory. The combination of film and theory which had been imagined by Paddy Whannel and designed by Peter Wollen found a rigorous and exhaustive voice within the pages of *Screen*. The connections with the *New Left Review* were both explicit – Ben Brewster, Alan Lovell and Peter Wollen spent time on both editorial boards – and implicit in the journal's policy of translating Marxist texts which had largely not been translated for Anglophone audiences. But other influences came from France: *Cahiers du Cinéma* and *Tel Quel*, the avant-garde journal which heavily featured work from Barthes, Jacques Derrida, Julia Kristeva and Michel Foucault amongst many more. *Tel Quel* represented a 'high point' of French structuralism, establishing an internal politics which both politicised and foreclosed the 'text', and the first edition of *Screen* under Rohdie's stewardship, published in spring 1971, indicated *Screen* was about to embark upon a similar critique. The editorial in this issue remains defiant and prescient: 'this opportunity must be seized by *Screen* to develop theories of film study, to analyse theories of education as these affect film study and by these operations help to define methods and techniques in both film study and film education. This emphasis in *Screen* on theory is crucial'.[22] Rohdie follows this with a declarative essay entitled 'Education and criticism: Notes on work to be done'.[23] 'Auteurs are out of time,' asserts Rohdie, 'the theory which makes them sacred makes no inroad on vulgar history, has no concepts for the social or collective or the national.' This provided the rationale for *Screen*: a rigorous approach to questioning film education and criticism. Rohdie, in particular, positions himself as an authoritative intellectual, speaking with great moral authority on the state of film education in Britain without necessarily having the expertise to make such pronouncements, other than his editorship of the journal. But Rohdie's editorials from this time read now like manifestos, pleading for theory even though it is not quite clear as to specifically *which theory* was required at this point. Rohdie was clearly influenced by both the events of May 1968 and the

22 'Editorial', *Screen* 12, no. 1 (Spring 1971): pp. 4–5.

23 Sam Rohdie, 'Education and Criticism: Notes on Work to Be Done', *Screen* 12, no. 1 (Spring 1971): pp. 9–13.

uncompromising approach taken by the *New Left Review* – a position which was to take *Screen* journal even further away from the wider work being undertaken by the BFI Educational Advisory Service.

This spring 1971 edition of *Screen* is also notable for the work undertaken by other figures, soon to become central to the *Screen* project. Ben Brewster reviewed the publication of the papers from the infamous Johns Hopkins Conference on the 'Languages of Criticism and the Sciences of Man' whereby Jacques Derrida shocked both attendees and fellow speakers with his sweeping take on structuralism.[24] Brewster's review immediately imports a constellation of French theory into *Screen*, casually referencing Althusser, Barthes, Derrida, Lacan and Foucault, and pointing another way forward for the *Screen* project, providing references to theorists whose work was, in many cases, not yet translated for Anglophone readers – in a manner reminiscent of Peter Wollen's inaugural BFI Education Seminar lectures. The result was a new field of research being shaped through the 'capturing' of different intellectual resources – one which was to continue throughout the 1970s. Furthermore, the issue offered a comprehensive takedown of contemporary British film criticism from Claire Johnston who provided an overview of film journals in Britain and France.[25] Johnston's charge was, by now, quite familiar: Britain was a provincial backwater compared to its sophisticated cross-channel neighbours. *Sight and Sound* was, again, the bogeyman, representing the 'bourgeois ideology' in communicating facts and values but refusing to explain why. *Movie* magazine was castigated for retaining a 'Leavisian method' of analysis while *Brighton Film Review* lacked 'a critical policy'. Johnston's review was a spiky intellectual intervention and clearly looked towards a very different future for *Screen*, the BFI and film studies in Britain.

## *Screen* theory

What is striking now is the delinquency of *Screen* journal. It offered a largely negative glimpse of contemporary film education and criticism in Britain but

24 Ben Brewster, 'Structuralism in Film Criticism', *Screen* 12, no. 1 (Spring 1971): pp. 49–58.

25 Claire Johnston, 'Film Journals; Britain and France', *Screen* 12, no. 1 (Spring 1971): pp. 49–56. See also Rachel Fabian's exemplary account of Johnston's work: 'Reconsidering the Work of Claire Johnston', *Feminist Media Histories* 4, no 3 (Summer 2018): pp. 244–73.

did not yet offer a remedy – aside from the import of continental theory. These theories, emerging from the constellation of Western Marxism pinpointed by the *New Left Review*, placed *Screen* within a lineage of oppositional Anglophone film writing from the 1960s onwards. While *Movie* magazine had posed questions in the early 1960s around authorship, which were re-calibrated by Peter Wollen and the BFI Education Department in more directly theoretical terms, *Screen* took this further and aligned theory to forms of practice, namely education and production. In this instance, the work of Louis Althusser was a major influence on *Screen*'s theoretical development, particularly his essay on 'Ideological State Apparatuses'.[26] The foregrounding of ideology in Althusser's work not only lay the groundwork for the introduction of Lacanian psychoanalysis, but was crucial in that Althusser afforded *Screen* intellectuals a language to speak about the production of imagery in cinema and to view it as part of a much wider apparatus, and one which produced ideological subjects. Althusser was also crucially important for those working in institutions in that his theories enabled a form of positioning which was deeply political – whatever institution one works in, irrespective of where one works in the institution, there is a form of politics specific to it. Althusser served as an example whereby one could 'struggle within various institutions, particularly institutions of education, without necessarily taking up positions automatically designated as left by some outside political agency … Althusser enabled one to take institutions and ideas seriously while still genuinely retaining a belief in the reality of class struggle and revolution'.[27] Althusser provided a conceptual space whereby the specific analysis of a form of culture, in this instance cinema, would maintain a conviction that specificity would be aligned with the fundamental divisions of capital and labour – along with the ideological formations which were enthroned in the reproduction of that division.

[26] Louis Althusser, *Lenin and Philosophy and Other Essays*, trans. Ben Brewster (London: New Left Books, 1970), p. 20. First published as 'Ideologie et appareils idéologiques d'État (notes pour une recherche)', *La Pensée* 151 (1970): pp. 3–38. There is a certain irony here – *Screen* was funded by the state through SEFT's grant-in-aid from the BFI and therefore *was* an apparatus of the state.

[27] Colin MacCabe, 'Class of '68: Elements of an Intellectual Biography', in *Tracking the Signifier: Theoretical Essays: Film, Linguistics, Literature* (Manchester: Manchester University Press, 1985), p. 13.

Therefore *Screen* journal, certainly in the 1970s, became so wedded to theoretical work that '*Screen* theory' became a term itself. One other thing is clear from the beginning: *Screen*'s political and cultural loyalties remained far from contemporary Britain, and the newly constituted editor, along with some important allies, was in search of intellectually engaged writers and academics to join his vision for the journal. Freshly invited on to the board was Colin MacCabe, a Cambridge scholar who had been attending lectures by Louis Althusser and Jacques Derrida at the École normale supérieure in Paris. MacCabe's tutor at Cambridge at the time was Stephen Heath who had been regularly attending the Roland Barthes lectures in Paris which had led to the publication of *S/Z*, Barthes's influential close reading of Balzac's short story 'Sarrasine'.[28] This armed MacCabe with a very compelling and up-to-date knowledge of contemporary French theoretical developments and he soon brought Heath with him from Cambridge to the *Screen* editorial board. *Screen*, again in deference to the *New Left Review*, also offered a whole series of translations in the early 1970s from historical Marxism ranging from Russian Formalism and Futurist texts on the cinema to works by the French film theorist Christian Metz – including an entire double issue of spring/summer 1973 devoted to Metz's work. This issue placed questions of textuality at the forefront of *Screen*'s concerns – Metz's 1971 doctoral thesis on language and the cinema reconfigured cinema as an arena where a number of codes and subcodes interacted in a textual system of cross-reference, each of which are manipulated into a flow of image and sound.

But *Screen* itself did not demonstrate original theoretical writing until the mid-1970s. Stephen Heath's extensive textual analysis of *Touch of Evil*, inspired by Barthes's *S/Z*, sparked a series of original English-language contributions to theory in the journal. But by this point, the politics of representation through Marx and Althusser and the textuality of Metz's work had been affixed to a controversial new theoretical source: the psychoanalytic language of Jacques Lacan. Lacan's work was thrilling for some readers, particularly within the women's movement. The reading of psychoanalytic texts allowed for a reframing of the questions posted by the women's liberation movement

28 Roland Barthes, *S/Z* (Paris: Editions du Seuil, 1970); see also S/Z, trans. Richard Miller (New York: Farrar, Straus & Giroux, 1974).

through this new vocabulary provided by Freud and Lacan which, in turn, made it possible to conceptualise oppression and repression. Lacan's work was first overtly introduced to Anglophone audiences through the *New Left Review*, which translated and published Louis Althusser's essay 'Freud and Lacan' in 1969.[29] For some, such as Laura Mulvey, this provided a pivotal awakening in her intellectual development.

> [Reading this article was] like waving a flag to Marxists to tell them: 'you have been taken in by bourgeois ideology in your attitude to Freud, and you have to liberate yourself from the way in which Freud has been taken over by American psychologists and psychologism and you have to look at Freud again'.[30] So it was in a sense directly addressed to Marxists and it was also bringing in the very complex relationship between Freud and Lacan within a couple of pages.[31]

It was through her reading of psychoanalysis which allowed Mulvey to view Hollywood through an entirely different lens. Mulvey says,

> The movies that I loved so much suddenly started to irritate me, and I saw them with different eyes … I was going to – well we didn't say 'feminism' in those days – a women's liberation reading group where we were trying to get to the bottom of women's oppression. We were reading Engels's *The Origin of the Family, Private Property and the State*, Lévi-Strauss 'Exchange of Women' and then we started to read Freud and a number of us got stuck and perhaps never managed to escape. Some of us went on to Lacan and got stuck there. Our reading group evolved and became a Lacan reading group which then produced the journal *m/f*, which you can think of as Male/Female or Marx/Freud.[32]

[29] By 1967, Lacan had published a mere two pieces in English. The first was the transcript of a lecture on the ego he had presented to The British Psycho-Analytical Society in May 1951, which did not receive any attention in the English-speaking world at all, save a vitriolic *précis* of its contents by the American psychoanalyst Henry Harper Hart, who took Lacan to task for rambling 'from Hegel to grasshoppers' and for descending into a state of 'neo-confusionism'. The other was a short book chapter on fetishism co-authored with Wladimir Granoff, which had in reality been written by Granoff alone, on the basis of extensive notes taken at Lacan's lectures and seminars in Paris. For more, see Dany Nobus, 'The Irredeemable Debt: On the English Translation of Lacan's First Two Public Seminars', *Psychoanalysis and History* 19, no. 2 (2017): pp. 173–213. I am also grateful to Dany Nobus for providing assistance in tracing Lacanian theory in Britain.

[30] Louis Althusser, 'Freud and Lacan', trans. Ben Brewster, *New Left Review* 1, no. 55 (May–June 1969): pp. 64–5.

[31] Anael Lejeune, Olivier Mignon and Raphel Pirenne (eds), *French Theory and American Art* (Berlin: Sternberg Press, 2013), p. 213.

[32] 'Suddenly, A Woman Spectator: An Interview with Laura Mulvey', *Another Gaze*, https://www.anothergaze.com/suddenly-woman-spectator-conversation-interview-feminism-laura-mulvey/, accessed 28 May 2021.

However, questions remained about the relevance of Jacques Lacan's work to film and film education. Lacan never overtly engaged with either topic. Yet for a period in the mid-1970s in *Screen*, his work was everywhere in the journal. These were, according to his detractors, a series of unproven assertions. His writings were not available en masse in English until 1977 and their sheer difficulty was off-putting for many of those engaged with film. There was a feeling that *Screen*, by this point, had veered too far-off course from its core function as a journal for film educators in Britain.[33] In late 1975, four members of the *Screen* board, Christine Gledhill, Alan Lovell, Christopher Williams and Ed Buscombe, all resigned in protest at the journal's presentation of Lacan's ideas.

> Much of the writing [in *Screen*] about psychoanalysis comes from a commitment that doesn't allow a critical distance to be taken. We believe that no socialist educationalist could be happy with Lacan's authoritarian account of the learning process…Lacan's position as presented raises many of the problems that have become familiar in discussion of F R Leavis's critical position – the refusal of a metalanguage, the attempt to explicate concepts only by showing them at work. Indeed, in confronting the use of Lacanian concepts in *Screen* we have come up against one of the special problems of Leavisite criticism, the use of terms whose repetition suggests they are important for the system of thought but whose meaning is hard to specify.[34]

Was *Screen* journal the place for such an overwhelming engagement with Lacanian theory? There certainly was a lack of communicative clarity in Lacan's work and this left a glaring lacuna between the premise of the journal and its application. *Screen* had apprehended a form of modernist écriture which alienated itself from any form of educationalist rationale. The gladiatorial approach to thinking and writing about film from a theoretically

[33] Jacques Lacan's *Écrits* was originally published in French in 1966 where it was an unexpected sensation in bookstores, selling 5,000 copies in less than two weeks. See Elisabeth Roudinesco, *Jacques Lacan* (New York: Columbia University Press, [1994] 1997), p. 328 – the heavily abridged English version failed to attract a large readership. See also Nobus, 'The Irredeemable Debt: On the English Translation of Lacan's First Two Public Seminars'. For more, see Johannes Angermuller, *Why There Is No Post-Structuralism in France* (London: Bloomsbury Academic, 2015), p. 69.

[34] Edward Buscombe, Christine Gledhill, Alan Lovell and Christopher Williams, 'Statement- Why We Have Resigned from the *Screen* Editorial Board', *Screen* 17, no. 2 (Summer 1976): pp. 88–109. See also 'The Avignon Papers', *Screen* Archive, Section 6/1 (1974), University of Glasgow.

informed standpoint had reached an apotheosis. The journal had adapted an unforgiving quality to its writing. It was far removed from the collaborative nature of the reading groups. The references to theoretical figures became a weaponised form of intellectualism, creating a form of High Theory which, as the resignation letter points out, was deeply hierarchical in tone. In speaking to two of the resignees now, their recollections reveals a split which may have corresponded to existing class divisions as much as cultural divisions within the BFI and SEFT. Christine Gledhill says:

> Well, I was very stimulated by *Screen*. I was frustrated when these pieces offered no attempt at mediation or introduction to an audience who didn't know that didn't know the context. Some of the ideas were very liberating. They did change conceptual frameworks and gave you a new way to think. I wasn't dead against the idea myself, but I think Alan [Lovell] was more concerned about the ideas themselves than we were. And being on the editorial board of *Screen*, there were obviously debates, Kari Hanet was there, Pam Cook was secretary with Sam Rohdie – it sometimes got rather intense. But it was a good kind of intensity in a way except when it got really embittered. Sam Rohdie was a very colourful character. And quite structured in many ways and not sympathetic. *Screen* had originally been a teacher's magazine. So, as a result of the discontent with the way Sam ran it and brought in these young men from Cambridge, who just talked as if they were still at Cambridge.[35]

Ed Buscombe, on the other hand, was regretful about his resignation – in fact, Buscombe was to resign from the *Screen* board on three separate occasions over the course of the following decade.

> Yes, there was a lot of heat generated. I mean, all left-wing movements have their schisms and personal feuds and so on. But there were also some issues at stake. There was a feeling that the people who were into Freud and Lacan and Althusser and all that had very little interest in what the BFI and the Education Department, in particular, was supposed to be about which was getting film studies created as a subject and getting it into classrooms, both universities and secondary schools. On the other hand, the people who were into these new ideas saw the opposition as just another expression of 'English empiricism' which was holding up intellectual progress. So

[35] Christine Gledhill, personal interview, 31 March 2023.

> those two sides of the argument were never really going to meet, I think. And *Screen* went its own way as an academic journal. and certainly, by being so academic played its part in film studies becoming an academic subject at university level. If you were in the university teaching film, you couldn't avoid it. Students wanted these hot ideas. Semiotics? Bring it on! I didn't feel like I was separate to [theory], but I didn't feel like I was one of the creators. There were some ways in which that body of theory directly impinged upon things that were of interest to me like authorship and auteur theory and all which I made some contributions to, and in so far as that theory had something to say about that, I was interested in. But I never could really get into Lacan. I thought this is beyond me. I don't have the motivation, I don't want to, it doesn't appeal, frankly. So, I allowed myself to be left behind on that. Metz, I had more time although he's slipped out of fashion.[36]

In essence, *Screen* was continuing the work of the BFI Education Department albeit in very different ways. In attempting to work through the intersections between different sets of ideas, culturally, ideologically, cinematically, it became apparent that some people had more of an interest in film as a pivot of this intersection while others were more interested in the ideas. Because *Screen* was still run by an executive composed of teachers, there remained a very real tension between the educators and theorists. In essence, these were two overlapping but different projects occurring with very different perspectives on how film education should be written about.

## Visual pleasure and narrative cinema

There is perhaps an irony that the journal, having been set up by men in order to create a force-field of theory within film study and film education, manifested its most influential moment on the terrain of the women's movement. Up to this point, every innovation within the BFI Education Department and SEFT/*Screen* had been within different theoretical sectors. Whannel had detected a carelessness in film appreciation and supplanted it with film culture. Wollen had enlarged this vision and annexed it to a dizzying range of theories and theorists

[36] Ed Buscombe, personal interview, 22 March 2023.

in order to affix film with a theoretical scaffold for study at third level. The BFI Education Department had expanded its remit to bring film studies to secondary schools, along with developing a remarkable range of theory-informed advisory documents for teachers and students. *Screen*'s scope, so far, had been to develop a discourse flanking each of these developments. The result of these efforts was a comprehensive and rich mural of film as a legitimate topic for critical analysis. But none of this work could match the impact of Laura Mulvey's short essay in the autumn 1975 edition of *Screen*. While the BFI Education Department was playing an important role in disseminating information regarding courses relating to women and film across Europe and America, feminist issues were a conspicuous absence in the journal until mid-1975 aside from an article in the summer edition that year where Julia Lesage challenged the phallocentrism of Colin MacCabe's writing in the journal.[37] But the autumn 1975 edition saw a change. It features Annette Kuhn's first published writing in the journal; a review of Claire Johnston and Pam Cook's book on Dorothy Arzner; Jacqueline Rose writing on J. M. Barrie's 'The Scenario for a Proposed Film of Peter Pan' through a psychoanalytical lens; and Laura Mulvey's first published piece in the journal: 'Visual Pleasure and Narrative Cinema'.[38]

Perhaps all of these essays emerged from the ecstatic feminist thinking of the mid-1970s through the collaborative spaces of the reading group collectives which we previously encountered. But so much has been written about Mulvey's essay, and much of it has disconnected the essay from both its production through the rigorous editorial processes at *Screen* and Mulvey's own personal situation at that time. 'I had never felt peripheral [discussing Hollywood films with] Paddy Whannel', says Mulvey now.

> But because I had an intellectual inferiority complex having left Oxford, not having coped with academic life, also having developed a complete writer's block, having nothing to write about and not being able to write anyway – it wasn't until later and through the women's movement that I started relating to the women's issues.
>
> So, my essay emerged after Peter [Wollen] went to Northwestern. I went too, with our son, Chad, was only three. This was a proper teaching post that

[37] Julia Lesage, 'The Human Subject – You? He? Or Me? (Or, the Case of the Missing Penis)', *Screen* 16, no. 2 (Summer 1975): pp. 77–83.

[38] Laura Mulvey, 'Visual Pleasure and Narrative Cinema', *Screen* 16, no. 3 (Autumn 1975): pp. 6–18.

> Paddy had got Peter. Peter had left Oxford with a third in English which was not really a passport to academia, even in those days. So, I was looking after Chad while Peter taught at Northwestern. It was around then that my deep love of Hollywood, which Paddy had nurtured for all of us, began to shift, in the first instance due to the impact of the women's movement. Those movies I used to watch with complete fascination I found I now watching with very different eyes. Through the women's liberation reading group that I had belonged to in the UK, I had come across Freud and then began to reflect on ways in which Hollywood could be read through a psychoanalytic perspective. But there was a new cinema emerging out of 16mm, too. 'Visual Pleasure …' really emerged out of those conjunctions, I didn't want to write an academic paper, though. Peter was always very supportive indeed, a very good reader, commentator, and editor. So was Ben Brewster, who was editing Screen at the time. He was amazing. I think Peter must have said 'show your draft to Claire Johnston and Paul Willemen and see what they say'. They said let's show it to Ben. Ben work on it with me for a bit over the summer of 1974. There's only one reference to Lacan, the Mirror Stage but I wasn't really Lacanian. I was more a straightforward Freudian.[39]

In tracing back, the editorial development of 'Visual Pleasure and Narrative Cinema', some fascinating strands emerge. Speaking to Alan Lovell in 2021, who was on the editorial board of *Screen* for most of 1975, he claimed that 'the first appearance of Lacan [in the journal] was through Laura Mulvey's article. And it was sent back to Laura to re-write, an editorial thing as it was confusing with the use of Lacan. She really brought Lacan more centrally to it. In my case, I was very puzzled.' A 2023 article in the *New Yorker*, celebrating the overwhelming influence of Mulvey's essay across the cultural sphere, also explicitly links the essay with Lacanian psychoanalysis.[40] But speaking to the key figures involved in the production and publication of what turned out to be a towering piece of work, a different story emerges. Ben Brewster was the editor of *Screen* at the time and says:

> I don't remember that Alan Lovell worked on 'Visual Pleasure and Narrative Cinema', but he might well have. At the time, work on each issue was delegated

[39] Laura Mulvey, personal interview, 6 November 2023.

[40] Lauren Michele Jackson, 'The Invention of the Male Gaze', *New Yorker*, 14 July 2023, https://www.newyorker.com/books/second-read/the-invention-of-the-male-gaze, accessed 2 June 2024.

> to a small group of board members. For that particular volume, I think Christine Gledhill was primarily responsible, but I vaguely remember that Alan was part of the group. The full board made basic decisions as to what each issue should contain, but the work of negotiating with contributors and copy-editing for each article would usually be assigned by the group to one member, and Alan may well have been responsible for Laura's article in this way. When whoever was responsible handed in final copy for 'Visual Pleasure' it was felt that the text needed improvement. The passive voice here stands for my lack of memory; I don't remember who felt this – it might have been me; it might have been Laura herself; it might have been Christine; it might have been Alan. I was assigned to do this re-editing, and again I don't know who decided this, though I suspect it was Laura (however, I suppose as editor-in-chief it was ultimately my responsibility). [Laura and I] had several long evening sessions over meals and drinks (we consumed the best part of a bottle of scotch in the process, I remember). The problems perceived were not about her arguments as such, but about the presentation. We went over the text line by line and paragraph by paragraph, rearranging and clarifying it rather than modifying the argument or adding to or subtracting from it. I don't now remember what the text we started from was like, or what changes we made, but I am certain that providing apparatus in the sense of notes and bibliography was never in either Laura's or my mind – it just isn't that kind of text. One of its virtues is that it summarises and arranges a lot of ideas that were in the air, without cluttering things up by trying to locate the sources of those ideas, though it's obvious one of the main sources was Freud (much less so Lacan).[41]

'I can confirm Ben's memory that he and I went through the text in the kind of close detail that he describes,' says Mulvey now.

> I can also confirm that Ben was enormously helpful to me. He understood the project, the lack of footnotes and bibliography, and he had a special 'creative sensitivity' as an editor. I can also confirm the bottle of whisky … I remember joking to Ben that perhaps Jack Daniels should get a thanks. It was Bourbon, and probably more of it than that half bottle he mentions! I can also confirm Ben's point that the essay emerged out of my engagement with Freud's very interesting attempts to understand gender in terms that echoed 'patriarchal' society rather than the complexities of the individual psyche. Apart from a passing mention of the Mirror Phase, there were no other Lacanian influences

41 Ben Brewster, personal interview, 10 December 2023.

> on the essay at all. At that point in time, I had read the Althusser essay in *New Left Review* – "Freud and Lacan" – which had interested me very much, but the ideas didn't translate into a Visual Pleasure essay influence. And *New Left Review* had also published 'The Mirror Phase' essay in the late 60s, which quite interested me although it was not so relevant to gender, which was my primary concern at the time. I don't think I encountered any more Lacan in English until the publication of *Écrits*, which I think was later [in 1977]. So, I didn't pursue Lacan pre-English translations – laziness perhaps, as I should have been able to read the French – but also not so relevant to the 'politics of representation' issues that concerned me then.

'In a way,' says Christine Gledhill now, 'I think consciousness is changed through contact with ideas. But not always in a direct way; some of the ideas, I think, opened out. That's what I always appreciated in what Laura did and why her piece took off so because she did translate it into women's experience. It's written in an enabling way and not in a way that is trying to dominate and telling you how bad everything is.'[42]

As Ben Brewster recalls, 'Visual Pleasure and Narrative Cinema' is an essay without footnotes. Its presentation can be compared to that of Juliet Mitchell some nine years previously whose 'Women: The Longest Revolution' was circulated in a similar fashion: both work exceptionally well as manifestos which cannot just be easily read but could be photocopied and widely shared. Mulvey's essay differs from the much of the work being published in *Screen* at the time, especially by Stephen Heath and Colin MacCabe, in that it is so explicable. One does not have to be au fait with Marxist theory in order to understand Mulvey's central thesis which is that the conventions of cinema reinforce patriarchal fantasies: 'the male gaze projects its figure onto the female figure, which is styled accordingly'. This perhaps explains how Mulvey's essay contributes to its position as being, in Mandy Merck's terms, 'by far the most cited work in its field, paradigmatic in cultural studies at large, ['Visual Pleasure…'] has been applied, elaborated, interrogated, revised, refuted, and endlessly reiterated in the years since its publication'. In this sense, Mulvey's work contrasts hugely with that of Heath and MacCabe; while all three writers are engaged with Lacanian psychoanalysis on the terrain of film studies, it is

42 Christine Gledhill, personal interview, 31 March 2023.

Mulvey who is most successful in challenging existing orthodoxies and utilising continental theory for a potential far beyond the pages of a film journal.[43] The radical energies of the BFI Education Department's work are released in Mulvey's essay as the boundaries between Hollywood and theory increasingly dissolve. Furthermore, while the subject which had been indicated by the male writers at *Screen* is often quite abstracted, Mulvey makes the subject more gendered, more concrete and more specific.

'I am very proud that I was sitting in [Laura's] house one evening because we all got friendly together,' remembers Jacqueline Rose.

> The early film scholars included Claire Johnston and Pam Cook, who were very vocal, very interesting, and many other women involved in writing about film and theory in different ways. Later there was *Camera Obscura* which came along in the States which was hugely influential as a feminist and film theory journal. But Laura was the pioneer, and I remember sitting in her house at a time when all these friendships were burgeoning in the early 1970s and she just ran past me the idea of the male gaze and scopophilia and voyeurism. And she just talked me through it, and I remember thinking 'this is incredible'.[44]

## Claire Johnston and Women's Cinema as Counter Cinema

As Rose attests, there were other important figures working within BFI Education and the women's movement. Claire Johnston had, by this stage, already produced path-breaking work in the field of women's cinema through her teaching, writing and curatorial work. Her 1973 essay 'Women's Cinema as Counter Cinema' is an essential text in tracing the development of dialogue around the topic of women's cinema. The essay, which appeared in *Notes*

43 An essay by Peter Wollen on Alfred Hitchcock from *Cinema* magazine in 1969 does point the way towards Mulvey's essay. Wollen's essay states:

> The act of watching dominates [Hitchcock's] films, both in the narration and in the narrative, in his style as director and in the relations between the dramatis personae. … To analyse his work we need … a concrete and meaningful psychology-semiology of gazing, watching, observing. The elementary terms for this are to be found, of course, in the work of Freud, in concepts such as skopophilia [*sic*] ('gazing impulse', voyeurism) and exhibitionism.

Peter Wollen, 'Hitchcock's Vision', *Cinema* 1, no. 3 (June 1969): p. 2.

44 Jacqueline Rose, personal interview, 31 July 2023.

*on Women's Cinema*, also published by SEFT albeit separately to *Screen*, showcases Johnston, a dynamic, provocative writer, who worked across numerous spheres as a filmmaker, film festival programmer, and activist.[45] Johnston was instrumental in bringing the works of female directors such as Dorothy Arzner and Ida Lupino into critical consideration during the 1970s while also avoiding the pitfalls of simply replacing one patriarchal canon of film directors with another. Her essay 'Women's Cinema …' signposts the way towards a theoretically rigorous form of feminist film criticism. The entire counter cinema pamphlet remains a fascinating and pioneering document in its own right, bringing together writing sources such as the First International Festival of Women's Films in New York, an interview with Argentinian French director Nelly Kaplan, an essay on Agnès Varda alongside Johnston's own essay. The arresting front cover features bold text and states that 'the image of women in the cinema has been an image created by men. The emergent women's cinema has begun the transformation of that image. These notes explore ideas and strategies developed in women's films.'[46] Johnston's essay fulfils an activist outlook as much as a theoretical approach, critiquing the 'dream machine' of Hollywood as reductive and deploys Roland Barthes's engagement with myth to point the way towards an alternative view of women in film, one which is far removed from the orthodox 'mirror image of real women'. The essay collection's wide-ranging assortment of feminist voices explicitly responds to the upsurge in women's film-making collectives across Britain and the United States in the 1970s, and, of course, the Edinburgh Film Festival's own Women's Film Festival in 1972, which had been programmed by Johnston, Laura Mulvey and Lynda Miles. 'Claire and Laura had very different positions', says Mandy Merck. 'Claire was more like a (Centre for Contemporary Cultural Studies at the University of) Birmingham position. She worked with a film group that made pastiche of popular entertainment with songs in it, and she did think that there were other dynamics than psychodynamics at work in women's subordination. She [also did significant work] on Dorothy Arzner.'[47]

45 Claire Johnston, ed., *Notes on Women's Cinema* (London: SEFT, 1973).
46 Ibid.
47 Mandy Merck, personal interview, 25 October 2023.

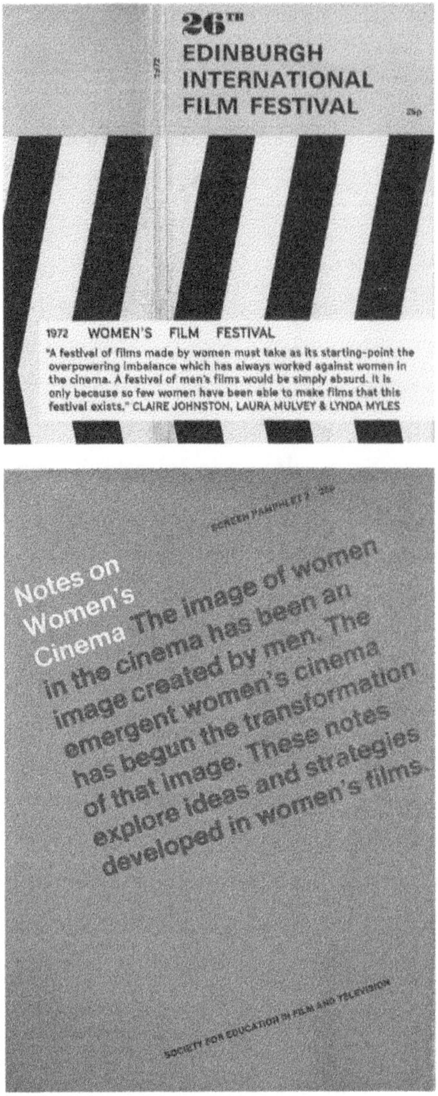


**Figure 12** (a) The 1972 Women's Film Festival, Edinburgh International Film Festival and (b) Claire Johnston, *Notes on Women's Cinema*, 1973.

'Claire was part of a women's group, we did set one up,' says Christine Gledhill.

> There had been two women's groups at the BFI: one that included Terry Lovell and Jean McCrindle and possibly Claire; and somehow that folded, and when I joined, we set up another one with Christine Geraghty, Angela Martin, Nicky North, myself and one or two others. So, we did run little courses. We had one set up at the Polytechnic of Central London. One was

> about images of women. That was quite good doing that, you were really trying to use the theory with women who were just interested but had no background, you realised how impossible it was! But I have to say, in those early days, there was a conviction you could change the world from [the SEFT and BFI Education premises at] Old Compton Street. That felt very achievable from the right film practice: Wollen and Mulvey's films, *Nightcleaners*, [Claire Johnston's] counter cinema, avant garde film – all these things [pointed] the way to change people's consciousness. And actually, teaching those [extra-mural] courses in adult education had really helped that.[48]

It is also Johnston's work with the Edinburgh Film Festival which demonstrates the vitality and immediacy of her work. Earlier in 1969, through the suggestion of *Movie* critic Charles Barr, the festival had approached Peter Wollen with a view to co-editing a book on Sam Fuller who was the subject of a retrospective that year. The consequences of this would prove to be significant for all parties: Fuller was soon afforded a retrospective at the NFT, and a collaboration between Edinburgh Film Festival and the work of the BFI Educational Department and *Screen* was activated through Wollen. In 1972, the festival announced a retrospective of another BFI Education Department favourite, Douglas Sirk who was also the subject of an edited collection by Jon Halliday, which had been published through the Cinema One imprint.[49] But more importantly, the festival director Lynda Myles collaborated with Johnston and Laura Mulvey to create the very first European film festival event solely devoted to female directors, screening films such as Leni Riefenstahl's *Das blaue Licht*, Leontine Sagan's *Mädchen in Uniform*, Nelly Kaplan's *La fiancée du pirate* and Jane Arden's *The Other Side of the Underneath*. Johnston continued to work on the festival in a programming and editorial capacity: the 1973 edition was devoted to Frank Tashlin, while the 1974 edition featured a retrospective on Raoul Walsh, another director with a body of work spanning a vast number of genres, including westerns, thrillers, musicals and comedies, and one who became revered in France. Johnston and Pam Cook wrote a piece on the place of women in the cinema of Walsh's work, using concepts borrowed

48 Christine Gledhill, personal interview, 31 March 2023.
49 Jon Halliday, Douglas Sirk, *Sirk on Sirk* (London: BFI/Secker and Warburg, 1971).

directly from Lacan. This featured in a festival publication devoted to Walsh – which was famously ripped up and thrown across a television studio by Barry Norman on *Film '74*, the BBC's flagship film review magazine programme. Lacan, it seems, had lost none of his antagonistic power. The following year, Johnston and Paul Willemen, a Belgian theorist living and working in London, edited the Edinburgh Film Festival publication devoted to Jacques Tourneur – the subject of that year's retrospective. Johnston and Willemen elaborated in their introduction that

> the Tourneur Retrospective emphasises the shift away from traditional auteurist retrospectives towards a foregrounding of the problem of reading and text construction. The retrospective does not propose a new author to be discovered, but a series of texts the reading of which will hopefully contribute to the clarification or formulation of important critical/theoretical issues in relation to the wider question of the development of a film culture.[50]

Paddy Whannel's term was still active and still symbolised so much: but what did film culture now mean? Did a film culture exist in Britain on any level yet? Or were Johnston and Willemen still overly reliant on ambitious theoretical work that was far too detached from practical concerns?

But Johnston's other work in the publication does point in the direction of an achievable form of film culture. Her essay on Tourneur's *Anne of the Indies* provides a study of the masquerade and femininity in Hollywood cinema, which is a riposte to the existing forms of theory in *Screen*, dismissed as patriarchal and one which does not take into account the 'asymmetry of patriarchal culture … under patriarchy we are condemned to live by our sexed identities … it seems in this respect Freud had a profounder understanding of femininity than the French analyst Jacques Lacan, from which the [Ben] Brewster/[Colin] MacCabe/[Stephen] Heath formulation derives, which in its formalism ignores the cultural forms and ideological realities by which we live'. This formulation did, in effect, have a presence at that very same Edinburgh Film Festival through a *Screen*-sponsored conference on the work of Bertolt Brecht. Colin MacCabe's notes on planning the Brecht conference remain in the *Screen* archive and offer an insight into the journal's positioning at

50 Claire Johnston, Paul Willemen, eds., *Jacques Tourneur* (Edinburgh: Edinburgh Film Festival, 1975).

the time. '[Does] Edinburgh offer a platform from which we can effectively intervene in the cultural situation of film?' he asks. 'It is my very subjective experience that there are many sixth formers and students who attend it for a variety of reasons who could be won over to a serious consideration of the theoretical consideration of film.'[51] The ambition of this proposal is quite remarkable – in reality, about sixty diehards attended the conference and there was an awareness that they were 'a small clique discussing abstract theoretical questions', as quoted by Ben Brewster in *Screen* the following year. Nevertheless, the Brecht conference provided the impetus for the final two Edinburgh programmes which Johnston co-programmed, culminating in two fascinating publications: the Edinburgh '76 and '77 magazines, the latter highlighting themes of history, production and memory. 'For the last two years,' wrote Johnston in her editorial for the latter magazine,

> [the Edinburgh Film Festival] has mounted special events which explored the image of cinema as an ideological practice. The Brecht Event … explored the question of film and politics largely in the light, posing the relation between the film text and the viewer as the pre-requisite for political questions in the cinema. The Psychoanalysis Event last year explored in great depth the question of the way in which representation inscribes positions to the posing of the cinematic institution in more rigorous terms … the subject of History/Production/Memory has been chosen as this year's special event [as] it consists of an attempt to re-think what we mean by making an 'intervention' in 'film culture' in the present conjecture …. Such work, it is hoped will open onto the possibility of developing strategies for defining the terms of an oppositional/'independent' film culture.

As Rachel Fabian has pointed out in her superb essay on Johnston's work, there is a consistency in her belief that 'theory should be continually tested and informed by filmmaking practice', which reflects her stated desire in the *Notes on Women's Cinema* pamphlet to establish a more worthwhile reciprocal relationship between critics or theorists and film-makers.[52] The scope of Johnston's work, particularly with Edinburgh Film Festival, offered a reorganisation of the practices encouraged by BFI Education and *Screen*

[51] Colin MacCabe, 'Notes on Possible Brecht Event', *Screen* Archive, Series 6/1 (17 October 1974), University of Glasgow.

[52] Rachel Fabian, 'Reconsidering the Work of Claire Johnston', pp. 244–73.

**Figure 13a and 13b** Edinburgh Film Festival magazines, in conjunction with *Screen*, 1976 and 1977.

through social and cultural experiences. In addressing film intellectually, but also in public, her work gave a different purchase to *Screen* theory. In effect, Edinburgh became an outlet similar to the BFI Summer Schools – in fact, both events often happened during the same month. But through Johnston, Edinburgh spelled out something far more radical than the summer schools. But Johnston's work at the Edinburgh Film Festival also highlights the primary concerns of the theoretical wing of SEFT at this juncture, and indicates a high point for *Screen* theory, one which, by the time of the final Edinburgh event, felt rather unstable as if it was about to topple in on itself. The plurality of her work though, across so many collective endeavours, is both remarkable in its commitment to her devotion to a women's counter-cinema and also indicative of a flexibility of movement by those working across similar fields at the same time. The radical profusion of Johnston's work was mirrored by Laura Mulvey and Peter Wollen who, by the mid-1970s, had also moved into making films. Their first film, *Penthilisea*, was made using equipment facilitated by Paddy Whannel in his new role at Northwestern University. On returning to Britain to allow Wollen take up his position at the University of Essex, they made *Riddles of the Sphinx* which took theory off the page and onto the screen. The film, funded by the BFI Production Board, was a staggeringly dense and often challenging address of the role of women in a patriarchal society. While not directly produced by the Education Department or SEFT/*Screen*, the film remains an invaluable document of feminism, formalism and psychoanalysis in action, as fragmented images and dialogue broke down the conventional narrative structures of framing and filming – the key structures used to objectify women in mainstream cinema. The experimental structure of the film ensured that it was ripe for interpretation – sometimes in ways which did not necessarily align with Mulvey and Wollen's concerns. But film was still just about on the cusp of academic recognition and, like those working within the field of women's studies, one simply had to be flexible as the security afforded by institutional recognition was still not yet fully realised and the BFI Education Department and SEFT/*Screen* provided integral space for key personnel to work out their rhetoric and activism under the umbrella of this quasi-academic, or proto-academic, space.

At this point, there were broadly two fields which had emerged from the twin endeavours of the BFI Education Department and SEFT/*Screen*: the educationists and the theorists. But there were also other divisions coming into view. 'It was a very male culture,' recalls John Ellis who joined the *Screen* board in the mid-1970s.

> And it was very difficult for women to hold their own in it. Christine Geraghty is one of the outstanding people who managed that because of her background in union politics. The *Screen* editorial board – when Kari Hanet arrived and breastfed her baby, that was a real moment of squirming! It was very funny. It was the male group who were really uncomfortable!

In 1977, Richard Dyer programmed a path-breaking season at the NFT entitled *Gays and Film*. The BFI Education Department also published a book with the same title, written by Dyer, to coincide with the event.[53]

'By the time I knew [the SEFT and BFI people], I felt they were very different kind of worlds,' recalls Dyer now.

> [On the one hand you had] *Screen* and Colin MacCabe and Stephen Heath even Laura Mulvey – one of the most delightful people in the world. They seemed intimidating, basically. And very committed to the idea of theory. I remember actually an event, a BFI event or SEFT event, that was about studying film. I gave a talk about textual analysis. I remember Claire Johnston was there and she was very unhappy because she said, 'you don't have any theory; you must have a theory'. And the theory was to be psychoanalysis. [There was a sense of] theory as a sort of fetish. But the BFI Education Department[still] actually had to deal with teachers and so on – so it couldn't just be all theory. I felt more at home there. Christine Gledhill was the first woman of any kind of seniority. There were people like Nicky North and Angela Martin who were very involved – even though I think they may have technically been secretaries; they were fully involved in the Summer Schools. I co-taught with Angela. Although most of the people in the education department with any kind of seniority were men. Jim Cook, Colin MacArthur, Ed Buscombe. I was very much an oddity in being gay at that time in that context. There probably was more – Robin Wood, for example, but he was not really in that world. He was absolutely in the world of film studies, but he was not much involved in *Screen* and SEFT or even

[53] 'While the *Gays and Film* pamphlet was written to accompany an NFT season – the season was not actually promoted by the education department, but it was through talking really with Angela Martin who agreed that it might be a good idea. And I think it was published through the Education Department.' Richard Dyer, personal interview, 27 July 2023.

the BFI. I was the only voice of that kind. Because *Screen* did actually review my pamphlet, *Gays and Film*, and the review is vile. It's really horrible. And it's horrible because it makes fun. I can take a joke [but] *Screen* was the most humourless publication that's ever been. And to have this jokey dismissal of what was, after all, quite an established political movement was really pretty awful actually. Until Mandy Merck took over *Screen*, it never felt [like] anywhere that would be welcoming to a kind of gay perspective. Whereas actually I don't remember doing anything specific with the Education Department around gay issues, I never had any feeling that they weren't comfortable, or it didn't fit in with their sense of what was good political and intellectual activity.[54]

## Theoretical collapse

By 1978, the project of BFI Education and *Screen* journal as a viable theoretical enterprise was in danger of falling apart under the weight of its own endeavours. Yet again, pressures were both internal and external and 1978 was somewhat of an annus horribilis for the theoretical project of *Screen*, in particular. A startling *denouement* came from a rather unlikely source: the Russell Harty show, a light entertainment programme broadcast on the ITV networks every Saturday night. The show featured Harty, along with writers Clive James and Janet Street-Porter as the resident sidekicks, offering pithy commentary on contemporary happenings in the media. On 23 September 1978, the show featured segments on astrology, R. D. Laing's soon-to-be-released debut album and a sneering takedown of the theoretical language being deployed by *Screen* journal. Harty's denunciation could have been taken from any time during the previous decade of the BFI's existence:

The [BFI] staff are split into left- and right-wing factions and the happy-go-lucky left of Marxist intellectuals are winning. Their theory is that the cinema isn't all that good for you unless it hurts a bit. They seem to think that watching films for fun is a sin. One of the most endearing traits is a tendency to talk and write in a form of jargon incomprehensible to ordinary mortals. Here is a sample from a journal called *Screen* which

[54] Richard Dyer, personal interview, 27 July 2023.

> regularly carries these contributions to culture...[A sample piece of text from *Screen* journal appears on the screen. It begins:] 'The hegemony of the visible without doubt informs the stress laid on the significant? of on-the-spot observation in the production of documentary films ...' before fading back to the television studio].[55]

Harty's quoting from *Screen* was a preamble – Keith Lucas, then-director of the BFI, was hauled on to the show, tasked with defending the 'incomprehensible' publications emerging from the institution's practices – Harty also brought up a silent film, funded by the BFI, centring upon the lives of a Navajo tribe in America, as evidence of the institution's reckless use of public funds.[56] 'The BFI,' boomed Clive James, 'is like a lot of good, left-wing institutions is peculiarly vulnerable to being radicalised. The radicals never want to take over Henley Regatta, they want to take over something that's already institutionalised. I don't think there's an awful lot left for the avant-garde to say.'

While the appearance of a film journal on primetime television may indicate a victory of sorts, it is difficult not to reflect on this footage with a certain degree of pity for *Screen* journal and their funders at the BFI. Dismissed by Harty and James as irrelevant remnants of a failed avant-garde, the journal was wildly out of context amid the light entertainment and jovial bonhomie of Saturday night entertainment. But where was *Screen* journal relevant? Certainly, the BFI itself was uncertain; the journal was under attack from the teachers and educators in the institute, but by this stage, *Screen* was imploding under the weight of its own positioning. The moment of *Screen*, of high theory, was about to pass. The investigation of psychoanalysis, politics, even linguistics, through *Screen* was fuelled by a belief that there was a way of rearranging the humanities, one which would produce new political insight or even generate a breakthrough of the moribund politics of the time. The pursuit of this agenda was the moment of *Screen*.

One can point to a specific article in *Screen* which announced the fallacy of the entire edifice. Written by Paul Willemen, 'Notes on Subjectivity' was

55 The offending text was written by Annette Kuhn and taken from 'The Camera I: Observations on Documentary', *Screen* 19, no. 2 (Summer 1978): pp. 71–83.

56 A special guest on the show was Anthony Alexander, political columnist for the *Daily Mail*. Alexander interrupted the proceedings to express how interested he was in the Navajo film; Lucas's attempts to offer more information on the film were curtly dismissed by Harty.

ostensibly a response to a previous article by Edward Branigan, but instead provided an argument which stated that any attempt to analyse the film as a text, which ignored the importance of the politics of the reader, was intellectually null.[57] The negative impact of the Paul Willemen article has been confirmed by a number of *Screen* writers from the time. Colin MacCabe wrote an article against Willemen but has since never included it in his bibliography as he now rejects his own riposte to Willemen. Essentially, Willemen had stated that any attempt to fix the status of the film text in a manner so that it could be analysed with psychoanalysis or linguistics was a doomed project. Nobody could come up with an answer to his arguments. Around the same time, Terry Eagleton also criticised the *Screen* project in the *New Left Review*, declaring that the formalism of *Screen* served to evaporate history which meant the 'historical specificity of the ideological codes' investigated was nothing more than a 'gesture'.[58] Elsewhere, sociologists Barry Hindess and Paul Hirst were developing their own critique of Althusser and of *Screen*, maintaining that if one was to truly follow Althusser's work, it would ultimately result in the rejection of every facet of Marx's own theories. Althusser's account of knowledge was denigrated as being 'contaminated by empiricism', a crushing denouement for any form of theoretical practice, particularly that of *Screen*.[59] Meanwhile, E. P. Thompson also published his own rebuttal to cultural and critical projects which are sympathetic to the use of Louis Althusser; his polemic entitled *The Poverty of Theory* criticised Althusser as anti-human, diminishing personal experience to mere consequences of economic relations. In Thompson's terms, French theory was elitist and only an elite academic cadre could engage with the Althusserian concept of reality.[60] But by 1979, the entire landscape changed overnight with the appointment of Margaret Thatcher as prime minister. But also, as film became established in the academy, professional recognition became not just a reality, but a rather attractive provider of security. Both Ben Brewster, who had edited *Screen* since 1974, and Elizabeth Cowie, who worked

57 Paul Willemen, 'Notes on Subjectivity: On Reading Edward Branigan's "Subjectivity Under Siege"', *Screen* 19, no. 1 (Spring 1978): pp. 41–70; 40–3. See also Colin MacCabe, 'The Discursive and the Ideological in Film: Notes on the Conditions of Political Intervention', *Screen* 19, no. 4 (Winter 1978): pp. 29–44.

58 Terry Eagleton, 'Aesthetics and Politics', *New Left Review* 1, no. 107 (January–February 1978): p. 23.

59 Barry Hindess and Paul Hirst, *Mode of Production and Social Formation: An Auto-Critique of Pre-Capitalist Modes of Production* (London: Palgrave Macmillan, 1977).

60 E. P. Thompson, *The Poverty of Theory* (London: Merlin, 1978).

closely on the journal, left in early 1977 to take up full-time academic posts at the University of Kent and the Slade Film School, respectively. 'Ben Brewster was sort of my hero,' says Jacqueline Rose,

> Because he worked for *New Left Review*, and he worked for *Screen*, he translated Althusser, he had a completely autonomous intellectual existence, and he hung out in Old Compton Street. I had just come from Paris. When he took his job at Kent, I felt the writing was on the wall. He had a huge influence on me getting my first university position because, before that, I had thought I would be a free-floating intellectual and be free of intellectual institutional affiliations of any kind. When he got the Kent job [and left *Screen*], I really thought times were changing, this really says something dramatic about how we all thought we could manage. He said to me don't live the life of a translator. You're always waiting for the next contract and most of them don't come true. And it's very badly paid.[61]

Brewster was replaced initially by Geoffrey Nowell-Smith and again by Mark Nash, during a period of great upheaval at SEFT. Numerous documents exist within the *Screen* archive detailing fractious planning meetings around *Screen*'s positioning and future. The board was reconstituted in 1979 and an internal paper, written by Claire Johnston in June of that year, expresses a wish that the

> isolation and marginalisation of *Screen* can only be counteracted by an anti-sectarian policy involving debate and a diversity of theoretical positions and ideological practices. The only real alternative is a schism of an even more serious kind that we experienced only two and a half years ago [when four members of the board resigned over the journal's use of Lacan].[62]

Johnston's tone was both positive and doom-laden. And as Britain entered into an entirely new political era, the work of the BFI Education Department and SEFT/*Screen* was to radically change course yet again.

Reflecting on the work undertaken by the BFI Education Department and SEFT/*Screen* during the 1970s, one is struck by the period's sense of major insurgency. The key figures we have encountered in this chapter working in

61 Jacqueline Rose, personal interview, 31 July 2023.
62 Claire Johnston, 'Screen's Historical Present', *Screen* Archive, Series 6/6 (1979), University of Glasgow.

and around the BFI were intoxicated by their readings and writings of the avant-garde, theory, and aesthetics and worked together in celebrating the crossover, the hybrids, the intersections of all these ideas through the medium of film. The 1970s were certainly an era of high theory; indeed, from the end of previous decade onwards, the period was crucial in witnessing the English translation of key theoretical texts: Jacques Derrida's *Of Grammatology* and *Writing and Difference*, both originally appearing in 1967, arrived in an English translation in 1974 and 1978, respectively. Barthes's *S/Z* (1970) was published in English in 1974, *The Pleasure of the Text* followed in 1975, *Sade, Fourier, Loyola* in 1976 and *Image-Music-Text*, a collection of essays edited by Stephen Heath landed in 1977.[63] Lacan's *Écrits*, as we have seen, was also translated with selections published in English in 1977, while Michel Foucault, whose work had arrived in England through the anti-psychiatry boom earlier in the decade, had *Discipline and Punish* and the first volume of the *History of Sexuality* appear between 1977 and 1979.[64] *Screen* was the primary outlet for the discourse around these publications, but also the centrifugal point for a great wave of intellectual excitement which was generated by the BFI Education Department's continuing work across film and theory. While the links between the institution and film education may have felt elusive at times, *Screen*'s work during the 1970s represents the belief, however naive, that re-organising the humanities through the grand narratives of Marxism, semiology and psychoanalysis which would produce a comprehensive breakthrough, or re-organisation, of the political. To achieve this, the aim was to put film at the centre of understanding the humanities. This moment

63 Jacques Derrida, *Of Grammatology*, trans. Gayati Chakravorty Spivak (Baltimore: Johns Hopkins University Press, 1976); Derrida, *Writing and Difference*, trans. Alan Bass (Chicago: University of Chicago Press, 1978). Roland Barthes, *S/Z*, trans. Richard Miller (New York: Farrar, Straus & Giroux, 1974); Barthes, *The Pleasure of the Text*, trans. Richard Miller (New York: Farrar, Straus & Giroux, 1975); Barthes, *Sade, Fourier, Loyola*, trans. Richard Miller (New York: Hill & Wang, 1975); Barthes, *Image-Music-Text*, trans. Stephen Heath (London: Fontana, 1977). For more on Barthes in translation, see Lucile Dumont, 'The Moving Frontiers of Intellectual Work: The Importation and Early Reception of Roland Barthes' Work in the United States (1960s–1980s), *Sociologica* (2017), doi.10.2383/86984.

64 Michel Foucault, *Discipline and Punish* (New York: Random House, 1977); Foucault, *History of Sexuality Volume 1: An Introduction* (London: Allen Lane, 1979). Foucault's reception in Britain is worthy of a separate full-length study, as he emerges through his links with the anti-psychiatry scene of the 1960s. See Colin Gordon, 'Foucault in Britain', in *Foucault and Political Reason: Liberalism, Neo-Liberalism, and Rationalities of Government*, ed. Andrew Barry, Thomas Osborne, Nikolas Rose (London: UCL, 1997).

of *Screen*, with its modernist pulse separate to what the journal published before and after this decade, is in pursuit of this agenda and it is a function which migrated from the wider project of the BFI Education Department in the previous decade. The department was often taxed with being insufficiently engaged with the real world of education and therefore considered unsound. But the configuration of the work analysed in this chapter speaks to both the political character of the age and continues to intervene, at a greater level, in the cultural arena of today, particularly through Laura Mulvey's essay. As we will see, in the final chapter, these tendencies did not entirely disappear as the BFI and *Screen* re-positioned themselves again for the more beleaguered political order of the 1980s Britain.

4

# The dismantling of theory

## A new decade

In the near decade since Paddy Whannel resigned from the BFI, many of the changes he had fought for had been implemented. Film studies was about to flourish as a third-level course across Britain. Primary and secondary schools started to take interest in teaching film as an adjunct, and Whannel's initiatives in developing a study extracts library at the BFI ensured that film could be used as a teaching aid in the classroom. A distinct film culture, his own term, had been realised in Britain; film education was not just established, but it had been situated in a democratic culture of its own and one which emerged in the image of Whannel's tireless work as a teacher, an administrator and, as Garry Whannel pointed out, a wonderful *animateur* of others. His resignation from the department paid tribute to his principles of clarity and conviction, and the ongoing work of the BFI and SEFT were testament to his vision of film education and his ability to make this a reality.

However, Whannel did not live to see the full bloom of these developments for which he had fought. On 8 July 1980, having just earned his first sabbatical from teaching at Northwestern University, Paddy Whannel died suddenly in London. His papers, which are kept at Northwestern University, paint a fascinating portrait of both his magnificent teaching – numerous letters of appreciation from his superior's pay testament to his work – and his continued engagement with contemporary developments in theory, but also his gradual ill-health. The final two points may be related. 'Paddy had high blood pressure', according to documentarian Mike Dibb, 'and later in life was hospitalised because of a brain haemorrhage. Nevertheless, he continued to retain his lovely Scottish sense of humour, and I heard that one day a friend of his came to the hospital and said, "Paddy, what brought this on?" To which he just looked up and smiled "Semiology!"'[1] But one can only wonder at Whannel's response to the sudden shift in the political landscape in Britain during 1979–80. The appointment of Margaret Thatcher as prime minister changed the outlook for progressive educational initiatives overnight. There was an immediate political intervention in state-funded institutions which threatened to extinguish the insurgent energy of the 1970s. These institutions were now required to have their activities vetted by government agencies, whereas previously they were merely questioned. If the 1970s can be considered as a parenthesis in cultural history, this parenthesis was now beginning to close.

'After 1979', says Laura Mulvey,

> the positive climate that had supported independent film in the 1970s began to change. Thatcher cut off a lot of funding for these experimental movies that weren't intended to reach a wide audience and would never producer value for money and so on. But, on the other hand, Channel 4 came on air in 1982 and offered different kinds of possibilities for independent film. But the 1980s was also a very rich period for alternative culture. Gay culture flourished; music videos began to be a site of visual experiment. And there was a very strong anti-Thatcher television through the 1980s – on all the channels, not just Channel 4. The 1970's intense concentration theory, austerity around 16mm and the materiality of the medium, kind of mutated into something else. For instance, the 1970s at Screen was very innovative, it brought in ideas that weren't circulating before. But the appointment of Mandy Merck editor of *Screen* acknowledged the way times had changed; she wanted to bring television and popular culture into the journal – and open it up so that it wouldn't be so dense and so French![2]

Much of the energy of the 1960s and 1970s was derived from a cleavage between frustrations with a moribund British culture and appropriations of a Francophone repertoire incorporating the nouvelle vague, Marxist and psychoanalytic theory, and an intellectual tradition steeped in the avant-garde. By the early 1980s, this moment had either passed or had been subsumed into other currents. For some, Paris had become too parochial a counterpoint. In

[1] Mike Dibb and Anneleen Masschelein, 'Ways of Seeing/Ways of Talking: Conversation and Collage in the Films of Mike Dibb', *Biography* 41, no. 2 (Spring 2018): 349.
[2] Laura Mulvey, personal interview, 6 November 2023.

1975, while lecturing in film at the University of Essex, Peter Wollen wrote an essay entitled 'The Two Avant-Gardes' for *Studio International* whereby he expressed a desire for the New York avant-garde to become more recognised within independent film-making communities in Britain. But it was also an attempt to nudge the work being done by *Screen* away from Parisian concerns towards a more cosmopolitan stance.[3] Wollen was perceptive in diagnosing a regression in *Screen*'s energies and looking towards a new cultural space for an emancipation from the tightly coiled theorizing, which was to undue *Screen* in the late 1970s. Slowly, *Screen* had to move towards a more radically pluralist approach in its concerns. The weight of the journal's gladiatorial approach had also exposed internal feuding to absurd degrees. An introduction written by Paul Willemen to a proposed *Screen Reader* in early 1980 was quickly scrapped after Willemen's text insulted members of the *Screen* editorial board and authors of the text within the reader itself.[4] Indeed, there is much evidence within the *Screen* archive of uncertainty as to the journal's positioning at the beginning of the decade. A planning document written by Colin MacCabe in 1979 expressed the need for the journal to 'open out' and to embark upon 'engagements with new areas of filmic and television practice and with the configurations of cultural struggle'.[5]

By the time *Screen* did open up, the publishing landscape was entirely different to that of 1971. An emergent cosmopolitan viewpoint was reflected throughout the myriad publications which began to flood Britain at the dawn of the 1980s. The emergence of magazines such as *The Face*, *Blitz* and *City Limits* showcased new intellectual and cultural developments, aligned with fashion and popular music and strands of postmodernism. Other cultural institutions such as the Institute of Contemporary Arts on the Mall in London offered hugely popular programming of talks and discussions with theorists, many of whom were first introduced to Anglophone audiences through the BFI Education Department and *Screen*. These institutions were able to benefit from the huge creative release

3 Peter Wollen, 'The Two Avant-Gardes', *Studio International* (November–December 1975): pp. 171–5. See also Peter Wollen, 'Europe and America', *Framework: The Journal of Cinema and Media*, no. 14 (Spring 1981): pp. 9–10.

4 '*Screen* minutes and accompanying documents', Series 6/7, *Screen* Archive (1980), University of Glasgow.

5 Colin MacCabe, 'The Future of *Screen*', Series 6/6, *Screen* Archive (14 May 1979), University of Glasgow.

**Figure 14** *City Limits* magazine. Design by David King. Courtesy of the Estate of David King.

**Figure 15** *Blitz* magazine, November, no. 26 issue. Photograph by Nick Knight.

**Figure 16** *The Face* magazine, issue 1, May 1980. Courtesy Nick Logan. Logo by Steve Bush. Photo by Chalkie Davies.

of the 1960s and 1970s, and there was a sense of emancipation as barriers between disciplines were broken down and channelled through new sources. The intellectual liberation, prompted by the BFI and *Screen* and the coming of theory, created a whole new cultural space, particularly within London. French theorists, such as Lacan and Jacques Derrida, were being name-dropped by pop bands such as Scritti Politti who released a single in 1982 titled 'Jacques Derrida'. Within a few years, Green Gartside, the band's frontman, was openly quoting Lacan in interviews with the music press. One could also attend the Institute of Contemporary Arts's talk series over the course of a year and hear from figures such as Derrida, but also Salman Rushdie, Kazuo Ishiguro and Martin Amis. In late 1984, the institute dedicated an entire series of talks to Michel Foucault. *Screen* alumni Colin MacCabe had made front page news in 1981 after being denied tenure at Cambridge after a dispute within the English Faculty of the teaching of structuralism. The popular music press featured writings by Paul Morley and Ian Penman, both of whom marshalled French theory to write about post-punk and new wave in a startlingly original, and often confrontational fashion. Later in the same decade, a non-academic music journal in Oxford called *Monitor*, spearheaded by Paul Oldfield and Simon Reynolds, was proposing entirely new possibilities for writing about pop music, filtered through the theories of Michel Foucault, an endeavour so successful that Oldfield and Reynolds were snapped up by *Melody Maker* and given free rein to develop their own theory-infused critiques of contemporary culture – albeit while writing about popular music rather than film.

All of these initiatives afforded film theory a new identity, one which was no longer entirely reliant on translation and presentation at the BFI or through *Screen*, but instead was able to merge with contemporary discourses around popular culture. This represents a reorganisation of the film theory field as a social space. The pursuit of theoretically driven readings of film was no longer consigned to the margins nor was the study of film. For some people working within the BFI and *Screen* during the 1970s, this provided an immediate existential problem: What was the function of BFI Education, and *Screen* journal now? Where do these insurgent energies go?

One continuing expression of this dynamic was on television through the advent of Channel 4 which began broadcasting in October 1982. 'I worked for SEFT and made several programmes for television', says Rod Stoneman, who was on the *Screen* board from 1980 until 1985 and later worked in commissioning and production for Channel 4 and the Irish Film Board.

> Employed in funding new films and programmes for ten years in [those positions], I found the complex structural theories I had encountered as a student and in the milieu of the *Screen* board helpful in trying to understand the process of film commissioning. The circumstance of *Screen* theory had opened a new schema of relevant knowledge which seemed to be pertinent and productive for the various innovative versions of film and television in which I was engaged. It offered necessary analytical tools in the close encounter with the underlying power structures of the media and ensured that entering a powerful institution like a television station was not too intimidating or inhibiting.[6]

## A new vision for *Screen*

By this stage, Anthony Smith was the head of the BFI. Smith was a current affairs producer, and the man who first floated the idea of a fourth terrestrial television

[6] Rod Stoneman, 'The Theory of Film Practice: Thirty Years Later', https://researchrepository.universityofgalway.ie/bitstreams/603a390b-3442-4cf4-b60e-41fa983fa3b5/download accessed 5 December 2024.

channel in Britain.[7] Smith was an administrator and intellectual in the mould of Paddy Whannel in that he navigated his way through considerable political challenges while heading up the institution yet still managed to operate under the radar. Unlike some of his predecessors, Smith was largely encouraging of any form of theoretical work being undertaken by the now-renamed BFI Education Department. Smith was well-connected – he had met Peter Wollen as early as 1955 as they both competed for an Oxford scholarship – and once appointed to the BFI, he set about plans to restructure the organisation's educational and publishing structure.[8] Meanwhile, Mandy Merck was appointed the editor of *Screen* in 1981. Many of the key figures from the previous decade had moved on. Some, like Colin MacCabe, were largely disenchanted with the theory wars, while others, like Stephen Heath and after a period of time on various advisory committees, Ben Brewster, fully returned to academia. Peter Wollen was lecturing in a variety of places, including Columbia University, where one of his students was the director, Kathryn Bigelow. But Merck's dynamic and pluralist approach was ideally placed to rejuvenate *Screen* for the 1980s.

7 Richard Paterson, 'In Memory of Anthony Smith CBE, Former Director of the BFI and BFI Fellow, 1938 to 2021', https://www.bfi.org.uk/news/anthony-smith-cbe-1938-2021-director-bfi, accessed 10 June 2024.

8 My office was on the floor beneath Tony Smith, and I always made a point of spending at least half an hour a day by the director's elbow to ensure our departmental policy priorities were at the forefront of his mind. And on one of those visits, his secretary came in, and said a courier has arrived from the Conservative government's Department of Education with an urgent letter for you. He opened it up, read it, threw it over to me, said have a read of that! Tt was from the senior civil servant at the Department of Education. It said, 'it has been brought to the minister's attention that a particular school of thought is dominant in SEFT.' And Tony was livid [with the government]! He called his secretary; he dictated a resounding defence of intellectual freedom! The minister in question was Rhodes Boyson who was a former head teacher, and an out-and-out Thatcherite. And the Governors, at the time, were suspicious of the Education Department's growing interest in theory. I got a terrible time from some of the Governors over policy papers. At the same time, I had a lot of support from other governors like Nicholas Garnham, Alan Sapper who was the general secretary of the ACTT technicians' union. When I got appointed to the management job, I had to attend the executive meetings and governors' meetings as well. I got this call from Alan, come round to see me in my office in Soho Square, he says 'I know you're a comrade' – he was a CP member – 'before the governors meeting, I want you to come round and give me the line!' He was a staunch supporter. But Michael Ralfe was one of my antagonists. And Colin Young was very hostile from a pragmatic practitioner's point of view, seeing the Education Department's concerns as not relevant to filmmakers. When he was appointed director of the National Film School, as it was then called, he consulted us as to the appropriate content of a filmmaker's education. He never offered any further comment on our views, which were close to that of the Polish Film School at Łódź with the emphasis on a broad aesthetic and social education but appointed a retired filmmaker to run a series of 'background' screenings. The headship of one of the Departments became vacant and Geoffrey Nowell-Smith applied for it. We had a long meeting which went into the night. Penelope was on the selection committee and Colin Young was too, Colin was adamant against Geoffrey getting the job, but Penelope wanted her dinner, so the job was offered to Geoffrey. Geoffrey bridged a lot of the Department's cultural and political concerns and he had good contacts in the wider culture."
Colin MacArthur, personal interview, 01 March 2023.

'In 1980', remembers Merck,

> there was a huge strike at *Time Out* that lasted from May till the end of August. The management by then were six or eight people including the owner Tony Elliott, who paid themselves far more than what we were getting. The management wanted to extend into publishing new magazines offering lesser salaries and conditions than those in our union agreement, which included equal pay and benefits for staff of all non-management ranks, from Deputy Editors to the Roadie. We fought against that. We lost. There was a move to start a new co-operative magazine which became *City Limits*. I worked on it from its inception in early October until January 1981. It was predictably unable to flourish. Tony really owned the entertainment listings market and its distribution. It had been possible for sympathetic unions to 'black' titles where journalists were on strike. Mrs Thatcher ended that possibility. By this time, I was sitting on the *Screen* board as this very naive person. The then editor Mark Nash had told me he was leaving soon and suggested I take over as I knew how to do production. And the head of the BFI, Tony Smith, was thinking of encouraging SEFT [the Society for Education in Film and Television] to change *Screen* from a quarterly to a bi-monthly. What Tony Smith wanted – and he told me so – was for us to replace *Sight and Sound*. I did a little of my own research and realised converting an academic journal into a monthly review magazine would be a catastrophe. But my film knowledge was very spotty, it was comprised of watching Sally Potter films and then watching Doris Day films and then writing about both. Colin MacCabe had left the Editorial Board. Stephen Heath only came to one meeting, he wanted to do other things with his life. Isaac Julien was in the group as was Kobena Mercer. I was essentially a manager-cum-copy editor who had enough knowledge to stop really crazy things getting into the journal. And enough bolshiness to sometimes irritate the writers. But I always ran any proposed editorial changes by them. This is from January 1981 until about May 1988.[9]

Merck inherited *Screen* at a time when political landscape was marked by new tensions, or the illumination of old ones: Northern Ireland could no longer be ignored and the combination of Cold War anxieties, political upheaval across Latin America and parts of Africa, and the resistance to

[9] Mandy Merck, personal interview, 25 October 2023.

communist power in eastern Europe all contributed to discourse, theoretical and otherwise, about the contestation of power, the divide between north and south, representation of marginalised communities and of sexual difference. Thus, the *Screen* which emerged under Merck editorship is looser and far more engaging than its previous incarnations. The journal featured much less theoretical writing, much less Althusser and Lacan, and a retreat from the grand narratives of Marxism, psychoanalysis and semiotics. The journal also made room to accommodate *Screen Education*, which had been revamped a few years previously as a result of the ongoing conflicts between the SEFT executive board, comprising educators and the theorists. *Screen Education* had covered some of the more popular aspects of cinema, including stardom, narrative and the studio system and offered an approach which resembled the work being undertaken by the Centre for Contemporary Cultural Studies at Birmingham under Richard Hoggart and Stuart Hall. Reading this new iteration *Screen* now, it scans far more benevolently than its sister publication.[10] The journal's engagement with film alongside popular culture focused its attention on intellectual traditions of subcultures and a far more stringent engagement with ethnicity and class through not just film but also popular music and television. Many influential writers from the wider left had written early articles for *Screen Education* including Griselda Pollock, Simon Frith, Tony Bennett, Iain Chambers, Angela McRobbie and Ernesto Laclau. *Screen Education*'s output during this time was vivid and innovative in its own right, with writers providing primers on the work of Antonio Gramsci and Pierre Bourdieu, offering pointers on the use of *New Musical Express* in the classroom and photomontage essays. These more accessible, introductory-style

10 'Between *Screen Education* and the *Screen* people', says Mandy Merck,

> there was a considerable class thing going on between the psychoanalytic theorists and the cultural studies theorists. The former presented themselves as more theoretically sophisticated. [In taking over the *Screen* editorship], I was the naive broker situated cannily by Mark [Nash, the previous editor of *Screen*] trying to hold things together. And that was because I could see that there was relevance in theories of cultural resistance and popular culture as well as psychodynamic thinking (although I was somewhat disenchanted by psychoanalysis because I was then undergoing some fairly homophobic analysis myself. The Institute of Psychoanalysis wouldn't train gay therapists at that time, since they regarded homosexuality as a psychological impairment.) I also had friends from the cultural studies community, like Simon Frith, through *Time Out*.

Mandy Merck, personal interview, 25 October 2023.

articles continued to appear in *Screen* after the merger of the two journals. This alliance between the concerns of *Screen* and *Screen Education* allowed for an immediate import of new discussions relating to subcultures, ethnicity and class. It also made the journal less overtly elitist and resulted in a journal with far more directly in common with the teaching of film in contemporary education settings, and also with the BFI's own history of working with adult education initiatives.

'When the journals were told to merge,' says Merck,

> I was supposed to pull it together in one thing, publishing every two months so you could pack it all in. We didn't have a board who could manage that rate of publication even though it was enthusiastic about and was far more eclectic that its predecessors. And we didn't have yet the reputation to do it. From 1981 we did have had a grant from the Arts Council to put in photo essays. So, all those famous postmodernist photographers, Cindy Sherman et al, they all went into *Screen*. We had some [articles on] television. And we did more things about race because Isaac Julien and Kobena were particularly enthusiastic and so was Annette Kuhn who was into Third Cinema. And with board members like Simon Watney, homosexuality entered, more as content than analysis – that provided another viewpoint.[11]

Reading *Screen* from the 1980s now, one is struck by how much more open the journal is – bordering on interactive. Merck maintained genial relations with SEFT although the work was still marked by stress.

> I slightly changed things which pissed people off all over the world. I included a line of intro after the title of each article, but people thought that was really crass. I once missed out a photo credit on a Mary Ann Doane piece and she didn't speak to me for about twenty-five years! And it was hard to do. At the end of my first year, I got pneumonia badly. The stress of editing *Screen* was terrifying. Ben Brewster would come in with tiny, tiny frames, not even enlargements, from The *Gay Shoe Clark* in 1903 or whatever and would want me to pull it together into a set of illustrations. It was scary.[12]

11 Mandy Merck, personal interview, 25 October 2023.
12 Ibid.

The fusion of *Screen* and *Screen Education* promised broader editorial address and an increased topicality of issues relating to sexuality.[13] However, the *Screen* of the 1980s did not shy away from engaging with contentious issues. The 'Difference and Its Discontents' issue of January 1987 offered an incendiary take on the silences of 'sexual difference' and its inability to theorise homosexuality.[14] The entire issue brought together writings from Mary Kelly, Jackie Stacey and Yve Lomax arguing against the psychodynamic ambit which posited sexual difference as a mere binary opposition, and the over-reliance on psychoanalytic theories of subjectivity which pose the feminine through 'lack' and 'absence' citing Stephen Heath's 1978 *Screen* essay 'Difference' which challenged Lacan's binary use of sexual difference. *Screen*'s engagement with queer theory was typically innovative and courageous.

> By the mid 1980s, the theory of biological sexual dualism was being challenged by semiotics and psychoanalysis, so that sexual 'difference' could be seen as non-biological. But it was still articulated in the traditional binary and implicitly heterosexual division. 'Same Difference' as someone said in the *Screen* issue I edited on 'Difference and its Discontents', which is the major source on all this. One manifestation of that was the French psychoanalytic position that trans people were refusing the binary and trying to be both sexes – see, for example, Catherine Millot's *Hors-Sexe*. Another, evident at a conference I attended in Southampton in 1986, was the complete omission of a LGB (T wasn't discussed there, I think) perspective on sexual difference. So, there were no panels on homosexuality and the prominent gay academics present, notably Jonathan Dollimore and Alan Sinfield, spoke instead on a panel on masculinity. Eve Sedgwick was present at the conference, having already published 'Between Men'. When I asked her to the gay lunchtime meeting some of us arranged in protest, she said, 'I have to point out that I am not gay.' Can't remember whether she came to it.[15]

13 A letter from the American film scholar B. Ruby Rich in the *Screen* archive congratulates Merck on making the journal 'fantastic, most especially as compared to its former self, but even independent of that' and particularly highlighted a Nicholas Garnham article as 'the best thing I've read on television and has given me some much-needed arguments for this debate over here'. 'Letter from B. Ruby Rich', *Screen* Archive, Series 6/12 (1985), University of Glasgow.

14 Mandy Merck, 'Introduction – Difference and Its Discontents', *Screen* 28, no.1 (Winter 1987): pp. 2–9. See also *The Sexual Subject: A Screen Reader in Sexuality* (London: Routledge, 1992).

15 Mandy Merck, personal interview, 4 June 2024. See also Catherine Millot, *Hors-sexe* (Paris: Point Hors Ligne, 1983).

While there was still a relative lack of articles specifically related to film pedagogy – largely because these articles lacked the rigour found elsewhere in the journal, this iteration of *Screen* was far more heterogeneous than is perhaps realised.[16] Along with its increased focus upon queer theory, the journal also deployed semiology to more immediate effect through an increased awareness and critique of racial and colonial codes. There was an entire issue dedicated to 'Racism, Colonialism, and the Cinema' featuring influential essays on representation by Robert Stam and Louise Spence and analyses of cinemas of the Global South, particular through Teshome H. Gabriel's 'Teaching Third World Cinema' which sets in motion a form of decoding specific to films emerging from Africa. The 1980s iteration of *Screen* offers a fundamental break with its austere theorising of the previous decade. It is far more attuned to what we would now call Cultural Studies and benefits from an increased focus upon specific social and historical contexts. But the culture of intellectual exchange still found new possibilities through the promise of production. Channel 4 had provided a real opportunity for people who had become familiar with theory through film studies initially in the art schools or had learned about theory second-hand through BFI Education and *Screen*, and had had their approach formed by it.[17] This meant that much of the intellectual energy generated by BFI Education and *Screen* wasn't dissipating, as such, it was merely being directed to new, alternative sources of radical exposure.

> People who had been radical scholars at *Screen* like John Ellis and Colin MacCabe had pushed for the foundation of Channel 4 and to have an independent production section in it. And they got their wish. And people I knew immediately began to work for it like Sue Clayton and Jonathan

[16] Terry Bolas, *Screen Education* (Bristol: Intellect, 2008), pp. 302–3.

[17] 'The whole thing about workshops and Channel Four had come out of the Independent Filmmakers Association which. had addressed the culture, the dying days of the Labour government in 1978/79 with a proposal which was re-purposed because Marc Karlin and said you really should pay attention to this fourth channel thing – there's a real opportunity there. They should be funding it out of all this television money slushing around and not this cinema culture which was ceased to exist. He was in the Berwick Street Collective, which was a lovely guy, one of those great native thinkers. I stayed on nominally on *Screen*. I was the one who suggested Mandy Merck become editor which was very left of field for those lads. By 1982, Simon Hartog, Keith Griffiths, Stuart Hood, and I proposed to do a regular programme for Channel 4 about cinema, addressing what was on in cinema or what could potentially see. It was completely blue-sky stuff, this exotic mix in a magazine programme. Pretty late in the day, they said can you do a pilot. So, we kind of threw together a pilot – and then we got the commission. No one else proposed to do anything like it.' (John Ellis, personal interview, 26 January 2023)

> Curling. The SEFT Education Officer Rod Stoneman became the Independent Commissioning Editor Alan Fountain's assistant. John Ellis made 'Visions' for many years which a series on film. And I had meanwhile had a friend, who got caught up in the current of young women being employed in Channel 4. She had been at Goldsmiths, she went right in, her name was Clare Beaven, and she had been making documentary stuff for various companies that furnished Channel 4, and she had been asked whether she wanted to submit a proposal for a season framing some Gay and Lesbian programmes that had already been commissioned, among them Isaac Julien's film *Looking For Langston* which was on the Harlem Renaissance. There was also a Stuart Marshall radical film called *Desire* and some more accessible docs as well. The idea was that we would build a series of 50-minute programmes around these 50-minute documentaries, adding other elements or even full programmes of smaller elements that we would commission or make. We did this for two 10-week programmes that aired in 1989 and 1990. The series went out on Tuesday which became the name of the programme [*Out On Tuesday*]. We didn't care about the straight community and that's what worked. Straight people were really perplexed why we weren't explaining ourselves, why we weren't cosseting them. We completely ignored the straight audience, which predictably loved the series. It was in the midst of Clause 28, which prohibited the 'promotion' of homosexuality in schools and local authorities. So we opened on Valentine's Day 1989 with a programme about whether or not it was possible to 'promote' homosexuality. Saatchi and Saatchi agreed to devise an ad campaign for the first programme, complete with a lesbian commercial. Next day the press was barraging Downing Street, and we had a hit.[18]

## The closure of *Screen*

But at an institutional level, the debates were less about sexual difference and representation, and more concerned with the demands for media studies to become an entitlement for students across primary and secondary sectors.[19]

[18] Mandy Merck, personal interview, 23 October 2023.

[19] An undated note from Peter Wollen in his archive is scathing about the development of media studies.

> 'The shift towards media studies is perilous', he says. 'The context should be semiotics (of iconic discourse texts) i.e. the necessary broadening through semiotics is more

*Screen* was still operating under the auspices of SEFT which had continued its work in servicing the needs and education of teachers working with film and television, and its summer schools continued throughout the decade whereby one could develop your knowledge of media sociology, create tape slide presentations, work with desktop publishing to create print media or even simulate the pressures of a newsroom in a television studio. But SEFT was suffering from a lack of a clear identity, separate to that of BFI Education. Both SEFT and *Screen* were also engaged in debates about their own relevance in the new media landscape. Some education commentators, such as David Buckingham, argued for a return to 'major theoretical debates' in *Screen* which would re-think 'the theoretical basis of educational practice' to encourage relationships between 'theory' and 'learning'.[20] And while *Screen* still received funding from the BFI, new sources of funding were being sought from the mid-1980s onwards as the journal debated its own relevancy. Some proposals suggested re-structuring the journal as a magazine in the style of *New Statesman* and *Marxism Today*, covering contemporary film releases, radical work on Channel 4 and developments in media studies.[21]

The major projects of BFI Education and SEFT of the 1960s and 1970s were the establishment of a theoretical discourse about film and television which challenged dominant discourses and the creation of an educational framework through which the serious study of film could be realised. But the massive exponential expansion of the academic industry aligned with the success of the pump-priming project led to the existential, and soon financial, crises engulfing *Screen* and SEFT. What was its function? Who was it working for – film educators, media studies teachers, the development of media education policy? The function of BFI Education and SEFT/*Screen*'s mere existence were coming under increasing threat as the decade ended and the importance of media education started to muscle in on SEFT's territory. The BFI became interested in working with primary schools, through the advocacy of Cary

> abstract – than media (dangers of empiricism). Film is a plural system. I am not interested in sociological bias (how to understand role of film or media in society. Centrality of film rather than tv rests … on quality (cf literature v journalism).'

Untitled document, PWO 4-1, Peter Wollen Archive, British Film Institute.

20 David Buckingham, personal interview, 7 August 2023.

21 Ed Buscombe, 'Topical Issues in *Screen*', *Screen* Archive, Series 6/9 (1982), University of Glasgow.

Bazalgette, and the department became central to the huge debates around education in the late 1980s, and the decision to create a national curriculum. While studying the media, either as part of film studies or as part of English and sociology, was a task which once had to be justified, it was now clear – particularly after the Conservative government, anxious about the influence of television on young people in Britain, commissioned a report from Her Majesty's Inspectorate (HMI) of Schools which concluded that 'specialist courses in media are not enough: all teachers should be involved in examining and discussing television programmes with young people'.[22] The BFI Education Department immediately set to work on engaging with mainstream education initiatives, setting up working groups of teachers and academics to define media education for young people. This work coincided with the government's decision to introduce a National Curriculum for England, Wales and Northern Ireland – which used the BFI's definitions of media education and declared that 'television and film and video form substantial elements of children's experience out of school which teachers must consider. Our assumption is that children should have the opportunity to apply their critical faculties to these major parts of contemporary culture.'[23]

In June 1986, SEFT and the HMI sponsored a meeting of parents, broadcasters and educators – including Cary Bazalgette from the BFI Education Department – at the BBC's Pebble Mill Studios in Birmingham to debate the current stage of media education. Many of the teachers involved were English teachers, familiar with the canon of English literature, but they had also encountered the contemporary developments around semiotics and linguistics through the works which had been disseminated first in Anglophone circles by the BFI Education Department – and the Centre for Contemporary Studies in Birmingham – during the previous decades. This curious position forced BFI Education and SEFT to confront both its past and future through the media education movement. But there was also competition from outside the institutions. In lobbying for film and media to become part of the curriculum, this opened up a whole new catchment area of teachers who

22 See Cary Bazalgette, ed., *Report of the Commission of Inquiry into English: Balancing Literature, Language and Media in the National Curriculum* (London: BFI, 1994).

23 Ibid.

would not have previously been part of this film education rubric. The BFI also funded advisory teachers within Local Educational Authorities at this point which further bolstered these efforts.[24]

SEFT differed from BFI Education in that it was essentially an independent organisation which meant it could act without institutional constraints and without fear of causing political embarrassment – unlike any official wing of the BFI. In fact, this fierce independence of spirit allowed *Screen* to operate in such a vociferous manner throughout the period covered by this book. But *Screen* itself, which remained largely aloof from the media education concerns being debated by the BFI Education Department itself, was in considerable trouble. The BFI was threatening to cut SEFT's grant, and the institution's work was sliding under the radar. *Screen* had actively engaged in a policy of 'self-criticism' throughout the decade, a policy which was largely lacking in the 1970s. By 1985, the journal had started to consider funding from areas other than the BFI, particularly as journals such as *Framework* and publishing ventures such as Comedia were now largely competitors in the field. The division of work between the *Screen* board and the SEFT board also remained uncomfortably wide and different constituencies of readers for *Screen* were emerging. The journal had a considerable following in North America and

24 Ian Wall, personal interview, 13 September 2023. Wall continues:

> The theoretical element was still very strong. I came to film studies with a Leavisite background. And then you get semiotics, ideology. Where do you go? They were brand new ideas. I did a workshop at the National Association of Teachers of English and the whole thing revolved around twelve-to-fourteen people in a workshop. I photocopied critical articles, some from the *Screen Readers*, and we screened *The China Syndrome*, I asked everyone to choose a theoretical paper [from the *Screen Readers*] and critique *The China Syndrome* from that theoretical viewpoint. Some people had a good Marxist view, some structuralist viewpoint, some were deconstructionist, some used Barthes and it really sparked a lot of debate within that group. From a classroom perspective, how do you introduce those things in a manageable way? We worked with SEFT and funded a couple of workshops. Where has been the impact of all of that stuff? I think it was terribly important. All the A levels were ultimately rewritten. It was quite theory informed. I came into that world, during those schisms, at the right time. It changed the way I taught, wrote, conducted workshops. Critical autonomy or critical practice has [now] been lost. It's now all about how many A*'s can they get, and students just want to be given the tools to get that. The days of getting teachers together to contrast semiotics with something else – it's long gone. The ability to work with no right answer is long gone. People get very concerned when they look at a film clip and cannot find a right answer. And that sense of questioning everything which was around in the 1970s, 1980s and spinning into the 1990s is gone. When you talk about film study, in primary school or secondary school, what is the point of it now? Or is now just answer a few questions on things that are mainstream?

Australia, but *Screen* was no longer the primary source in Britain for the translation and publication of radical theories of film.

But there was also still quite a gulf between film theory and film criticism. The writer Judith Williamson, who was film critic for the *New Statesman* from 1986 to 1988, stated that

> this gulf [between film theory and film criticism] is neither necessary nor inevitable. Film theory offers not so much comments on particular films, but ways of looking at films which can be used more than once, as it were, going against the grain of the consumer ethic. Film theory offers not so much comments on particular films, but ways of looking at films which can be used more than once, as it were, going against the grain of the consumer ethic I would like to use this space to suggest ways of thinking about different kinds of film ... unlike many academic theorists I strongly believe that all really useful ideas can and should be expressed clearly. On the other hand, there is a strong anti-intellectual streak in our mainstream press; but the fear of ideas is only the other side of the coin from obscuring them.[25]

Williamson was commenting on a symposium at the London Film Festival on the Function of Film Criticism and perhaps some sort of rapprochement was being reached in terms of theory and practice: within a couple of years, Peter Wollen started to write semi-regularly for *Sight and Sound* and his own writing had long eschewed the forms of auteur-structuralism he presented at the BFI Education Seminars in the late 1960s. Wollen's own late style was than of an elegant, man of letters – and one who was no longer fearful of empiricism, or what it may represent.

Both *Screen* and SEFT were in severe danger by the end of the decade. Merck left in May 1988, initially on a temporary basis to pursue her work with Channel 4, and Anthony Smith left the BFI the same year. Later that year, an external consultancy review of SEFT was commissioned by the BFI and undertaken by Comedia. The report was described by David Lusted in a meeting at the time as purely, 'destructive', and he recommended that SEFT be dismantled. *Screen* journal, meanwhile, was put up for adoption with the John Logie Baird centre at the University of Glasgow taking over its operation.

[25] Judith Williamson, 'Viewfinder', *New Statesman*, 12 December 1986, p. 23.

Almost forty years after its inception, *Screen* had become an academic journal. Lusted now reflects that

> SEFT was an important organisation for both the *Screen* journal and its many educational activities but there were always tensions between the two operations due to budget restrictions from its funding sources, a BFI grant and earned income. In meetings of the membership in the days leading up to its demise, there were increasing arguments between those who wanted SEFT for the intellectual work of *Screen* and film teachers who wanted a professional representative body to argue their case. I was among a small group of members who argued for SEFT to continue both areas of work but in a more limited, financially sustainable way. But people in higher education rarely concerned themselves with the needs of the mandatory education sector nor even further education. And many teachers didn't have the time or energy to fight their corner. I was keen to join with others in reconciling the two sides, but a resolution was never found. That conflict wasn't responsible for the closure of SEFT, however. You have to look to figures in the BFI for that. Tony Smith was in many ways an excellent director of the BFI, probably the best it ever had, but he was guided to give SEFT up, to release the grant money for other purposes. There was always tension between the BFI and SEFT before it shut up shop. I was never part of that group of mainly Education Department staff who took on what was considered the over-theorisation of the *Screen* project, partly because I didn't understand enough to join but also because I was reluctant. That was the case right up to the moment *Screen* was hived off to academia and its teacher representation abandoned as SEFT was wound up. SEFT didn't implode because of internal arguments among its membership, as many argue. Before any possibility of resolution, it had its grant removed by the BFI for funding use elsewhere. That whole period of the 60s and 70s was a fervent of growth and activity advancing the cause of film studies. While intellectual work continued then and continues now in the university system, despite huge problems in the sector, there has never been an activist film teacher's organisation since, and it is one of the reasons for the many limitations to the teaching of film studies in the mandatory sector now.[26]

26 David Lusted, personal interview, 31 March 2023.

## Legacies and aftermaths

Since Paddy Whannel's appointment to the BFI staff in 1957, the phenomenal reach of the BFI Education Department and *Screen*'s initiatives expanded the scope of film study to previously unimaginable realms. But at the dawn of the 1990s, much of this work had come to an end. The extra-mural classes undertaken with the University of London had been taken over entirely by the university in 1983 and much of these courses were re-constituted as media studies classes. The BFI Summer Schools, so rich and formative for so many key figures within the spectrum of film study in Britain, were to be discontinued with the final School pencilled in for 1989 – coming full circle, the Summer School, held at the University of Stirling, was titled 'What is British Cinema?' and promised to offer a renewed critical engagement with British films, particularly in the light of Channel 4's successful production of British films. Even more presciently, one further summer school postscript – although billed as a conference – was held in 1991, also at Stirling, called 'Borderlines: Films In Europe' and promised to analyse the changing dynamics of Europe through identification of 'others' both inside and outside Europe.

SEFT was no more and *Screen* itself was, in some respects, no longer an outsider. It became part of the machinery of the academic institution where it still remains a hugely respected journal. Annette Kuhn, who joined the board in the mid-1970s and remained involved with *Screen* until 2014, argues for a conception of *Screen* which goes beyond its apparent heyday. '*Screen* was misunderstood in many respects', says Kuhn now.

> I was involved with *Screen* for a total of over thirty years, most of them after 1989, when the journal moved from London to Glasgow. I finally stood down in 2014, having been involved since 1976. I know that many people think of *Screen* as something that happened – or was most important-- during the 1970s, but it's still going strong and still publishing good work, as well as supporting promising scholars in other ways (with the *Screen* Award, for instance). I really enjoyed working with my fellow editors during the Glasgow years. We made a great team. The period from around 1975–1978 had been very intense for film studies, and I was still finding my way at the time. I had an intuition of what I wanted to do, though without knowing precisely what it was. Like myself, all the people you have talked to have

> had long and varied careers since the 1970s. In 1979 I was offered a job in the States on the back of being a member of the Screen editorial board. At this time I was doing part-time lecturing at the Polytechnic of Central London on a short-term contract. So I was free to travel to the University of Iowa for a semester to replace Dudley Andrew, who was on sabbatical. I suspect they thought they had secured the services of an *eminence grise* from *Screen* whereas what they got was someone whom today we would call an early career scholar. It was a fascinating and energising time – and there were other things going on in my life as well – feminism among them. It was when working in the States that I became inspired to write *Women's Pictures: Feminism and Cinema*, which came out in 1982, just as feminism and film studies were joining forces in what would become a highly productive relationship. Meanwhile, at Screen things were loosening up under the editorships of Geoffrey Nowell-Smith and Mark Nash, with feminist issues coming further to the fore when Mandy Merck became editor. My essay, 'Women's Genres' [on melodrama, soap opera, and theory], which appeared in *Screen* in 1984, is perhaps as important for me as 'Visual Pleasure and Narrative Cinema' has been for Laura, in the sense that it's probably the article by me that had the widest attention. It was actually a salvo in a series of debates within feminist film studies around Hollywood melodrama and the female audience, debates which were also shaping some of my teaching.[27]

While *Screen* continued its work at the University of Glasgow, the BFI Education Department also continued apace, although no less turbulently into the 1990s and 2000s. Cary Bazalgette, in collaboration with UNESCO and the Centre de Liaison de l'Enseignement et des Moyens d'Information in Paris, organised an international conference on media education which had far-reaching implications for the development of media and education across Europe. The BFI Education Department also worked with the Open University in developing distance learning training packs for primary and secondary teachers, and Bazalgette was very successful in directing the institute towards working with primary schools. But the incoming New Labour government was unwilling to do anything radical in education.

[27] Annette Kuhn. personal interview, 1 August 2023. See also Annette Kuhn, *Women's Pictures: Feminism and Cinema* (London: Routledge, 1982) and Annette Kuhn, 'Women's Genres', *Screen* 25, no. 1 (1984): 18–29.

The idea of working in a radical fashion with education, at an institutional level, does feel like an archaic notion. In an era where the very notion of the humanities is in crisis, cultural institutions are devalued and defunded, the history of the BFI Education Department and SEFT seems like a Hollywood dreamland story from an entirely different era, a parenthesis in history. But it doesn't have to be this way. These stories from the personnel who worked at such a vanguard of culture and politics and education point towards a way forward more so than creating a benign history. While many people do not necessarily want to re-enact the debates of the theory wars in the mid-1970s, we have much to learn from the intellectual commitment and curiosity which prompted these debates in the first place – and, above all else, the sense of the collective in action and its impact upon those who may not have had the educational opportunities, or even self-confidence, to engage with these ideas and concepts otherwise.

In speaking with so many writers and intellectuals who had benefitted from the Education Department's range of creative and pedagogic practices, I was astounded by the sense of openness, the collaborative drive of working collectively in the name of not just doing something *different*, but the feeling that it was going to make an actual *difference*, especially when it comes to popular culture, sexuality and race. From a contemporary perspective, the culture wars of the twenty-first century are precisely targeting these interests, except the extent of verbal and other forms of violences against what was considered as progressive in the 1970s has increased. The work undertaken by these figures working in alliance through the BFI was important at the time, but even more urgent now.

These alliances were new and exciting. Through the opening up of the universities for women, working classes and ethnic minorities, learning and education provided both the vehicle and the vector for this work. It had a vital, antagonistic energy. I got the feeling from so many of my interviewees of being on an agit-train, part of something entirely new, not entirely knowing what was happening at time, and that this, in itself, was sustaining. Everyone had a role to play, and many of these people were, in Antonio Gramsci's term, 'organic intellectuals'. They were often people who knew about power from having survived it rather than being awarded it. The work of the BFI Education Department and SEFT was unparalleled in forming an entry point for so many rich ideas and concepts, particularly ones which emerged from outside of traditional Anglophone culture. One of this book's convictions is that the intersection of these preoccupations around film, theory and politics represented a sort of faith in intellectual curiosity and rigorous thinking, but also a faith in the potential of the institution to inculcate change, and to operate at the vanguard in leading and directing that change. To consider what was happening at the BFI Education Department and *Screen* journal and to glimpse the inner workings of its people, is to consider the possibilities of critical thinking, attentive interpretation and how the humanities can play a role in cultural regeneration.

As we have seen, this approach to film and theory started in relatively small places: a seminar in the basement of the BFI Education Department at Old Compton Street in Soho or a summer school near a golf course at St. Andrews in Scotland. But the introduction of an idea or a concept in these places quickly gets drawn into a more influential role and starts to shape how we think and speak about film and culture in the classroom, lecture-hall and beyond. It was in these small places, too, that far-flung debates about politics or psychoanalysis emerged as seeds from which an array of counterpoints and arguments around cinema could be developed. A magnificent vitality emerges when you disconnect a theory from one cultural scene and re-connect it to another: the BFI Education Department proved to be remarkably receptive towards these forms of citation, appropriation and even apprehension.

But it was through the empirical and the anecdotal that much of the most fascinating material emerged from the book. The account provided by Laura Mulvey and Ben Brewster on the shaping of Mulvey's 'Visual Pleasure and Narrative Cinema' essay provides an enlightening insight into the editorial collaborations which served to present arguably the most influential essay ever written under the auspices of film studies. And the anecdotal also allowed some degree of light and emotion into what can be a very dry scene – Richard Dyer refers to *Screen* as the 'most humourless publication that's ever been' – but there was also emotion, evidenced by David Lusted and stated that 'the thing about being working class is that you never, ever believe you can do it. You need people to tell you [you] can do it. I owe a career and a life to Paddy

Whannel, and everybody before and after that. I'm immensely grateful for that.'[28]

The illuminating recollections and insight provided by these conversations cuts through the complex institutional structures of the period, allowing the space for a more coherent narrative amid the allegiances and affiliations which appear and re-appear throughout this history. The use of a wide range of interviews also swerves a narrower focus on individuals – although if this book does have an overriding figure of influence, it is surely Paddy Whannel. He was, for a period at least, enabled by a dynamic institution which supported his ideas and outputs, and did not interfere in his recruitment strategies. Furthermore, the BFI was certainly progressive in many ways when it comes to the role of women in the institution, especially from the 1970s onwards. Laura Mulvey, Claire Johnston, Pam Cook, Christine Geraghty, Christine Gledhill, Nicky North, Angela Martin, Kari Hanet, Mandy Merck and Cary Bazalgette all played essential roles across all levels of the Education Department and SEFT's output during this rich period. 'The women's movement had to be part of our thinking with Angela and Nicky and me there', reflects Christine Gledhill who joined the BFI in 1975 and worked across education and publishing until 1991.

> In the materials section, we started to collect extracts from women's films and the study extracts – there was no VHS in those days – the study extracts became very important resources for teachers who wanted to support a screening with other examples. And we made filmographies of women's films which was interesting because we had the problem of trying to put them into different categories. And then the bibliographies, Nicky and I worked on. So yes, a large element [of our work] was related to the women's movement.

But what of actual film? Where does that figure in all of this, or was it mere grist to the mill of theory and activism? Perhaps it's easy to lose sight of film amongst the transdisciplinary excitement of recounting the BFI and SEFT's work during this period. Yet on reading through internal documents, published pamphlets, teaching aids and through the interviews conducted for this book, certain films and genres crop up repeatedly. The films of John Ford compelled educationists from almost every era of the BFI Education

[28] David Lusted, personal interview, 31 March 2023.

Department and SEFT's existence and were deployed as rich examples prime for interpretation by advocates of both film appreciation, in the BFI's early days, and film semiotics later on. The work of film-makers such as Nicholas Ray and Sam Fuller provided a connective bridge between Hollywood cinema and more sophisticated ways of reading film. As we have seen, Laura Mulvey recollects the International Festival of Independent Avant-Garde Film at the NFT in 1973 as pivotal in her own intellectual development as it provided an opportunity to see films by Chantal Akerman, Yvonne Rainer and Jackie Raynal for the first time in London. There is also the overriding sense of community and collaboration, one which was oppositional and contentious at times, but provides the vector for this work across film and theory.

The legacy of all this is certainly substantial. Film studies was formed intellectually, and no other Anglo-Saxon country had the same impact – this explains why many American universities looked to the BFI as having a unique combination of resources, people and intellectual heft. But this work wasn't purely linked to the theory; it was also part of the real work being done in teaching, production, the making of film extracts available for teachers, the extra mural courses, the conferences and lobbying by the institute on behalf of film education. John Ellis remarks:

> There was a really strong tradition that was given a real push forward because you had the BFI as an institution – always a problematic institution – but less problematic in the resources it brought around education rather than elsewhere. BFI education was colonised by people out of Cultural Studies, the people who were to some degree dispossessed out of *New Left Review* because they were interested in culture rather than knowing huge amounts about the history and politics of a far-flung place. They had the instinct that something is happening in our culture and it's permeable from the left point of view and it's important for the future. They managed to pull something off and it was a substantial space of work. But to annoying degree it is being frittered away because it – I mean film studies – became a very separate area. That's the problem of film studies in this century, it made itself separate and has now become the target for all sorts of cuts. Whereas those people working in television studies, mass media and so on, are safer because they have adapted more easily to production now that it has become affordable and pedagogically respectable. So, film studies moved into television studies and television studies moved into media studies of various sorts. It's remarkable

> how few people have changed their position. 'What is the BFI's relationship to the film industry? And its relationship to the Hollywood presence in London which was always a noticeable presence. The film industry has a difficulty with negotiating its place as a cultural institution on a par with the National Theatre, National Gallery, and so on. Because the film industry wants that to happen and at the same time it doesn't. There was always the perception that it was being colonised by the Left – well, it was – and people sometimes didn't play that well. There is something else as well, their running of the archive and their broader cultural machine, they've never been happy with it. It's always been a bad place to work. And that is very odd. Maybe there is something like sick institution syndrome. For far too long, it was people fighting over crumbs. And the Education Department fell into that as well.[29]

Nevertheless, it is in this sense of the work being somehow social and practical as much as it was theoretical which this book has also attempted to convey. These elements were mobilised together in an enterprise which was astoundingly original, and which absorbed them. There is also a unity in the recollections in the collective sense of wonder and intoxication with each other's work. 'I remember being parts of discussion groups with Claire Johnston or just being in the general ambience,' says Jacqueline Rose.

> Paul Willemen, Claire Johnston, and Pam Cook [were there] and [I had the] feeling that they were pioneers in their way as well. They were doing something completely different to Laura Mulvey. They weren't psychoanalytic thinkers. But they were so strong on women directors and women in film. And that was a whole other tradition that they initiated in a way. I remember thinking how impressive they were. If you factor in Christine Gledhill who was another important presence, if you list all those women, something important is going on at *Screen*. I certainly felt welcome there.[30]

Certainly, the work of the institution brought together the different, spacious energies of the emergent women's movement and the plethora of activity through reading groups. 'The arrival of theory in *Screen*,' continues Rose, 'made you feel you were at the beating heart of a real theoretical moment which stretched from Paris to London and to the west coast of America.'[31]

29 John Ellis, personal interview, 26 January 2023.
30 Jacqueline Rose, personal interview, 31 July 2023.
31 Ibid.

This is the overwhelming feeling from this era: a massively progressive enterprise, one which was important, devoted to seeing things differently and changing things. It's important to note that the one piece of theoretical writing which has outlasted everything covered in this book is Laura Mulvey's essay on 'Visual Pleasure and Narrative Cinema'. It wasn't gladiatorial in the manner of other *Screen* writing at the time but was focused upon changing things and was an attempt to apply theory to something concrete. The theorist Judith Williamson, whose book *Decoding Advertisements* was a hugely influential and readable text which also applied theory to representation, reflects that 'all those feminist reading groups had theory behind them. They were focused upon changing things, examining one's role and one's complicity in one's oppression.' But, as Williamson continues,

> *Screen* put people off the idea of theory. It created a backlash by giving the impression that all theory is all incomprehensible – but it's not. Theory can be applied to real things and real life. There was something alive about that time. There was a sense of possibility: people were going to create an alternative. It was a time when you felt everything could change through the ability to think differently and not just accept things as they are. How does reading theory illuminate the mode of address of media – the way it binds us into particular ideas and attitudes? It felt very important to teach this. The enterprise isn't misguided or pointless as an anti-theory position would imply.[32]

As we have shown, the BFI Education Department and SEFT endeavoured to examine the role of film in the orbit of education, politics and history. The challenging of the orthodox modes of film's position in post-war Britain suggests a sort of blind optimism, where the heady mixture of theories and interpretations would provide the key to all the ideologies. Yet there are few institutions in Britain whose work, during this parenthesis of an era, come close to the work undertaken by BFI Education and *Screen*. Their work took pleasure in the intellect, and this cannot be easily repressed, no matter how much our present situation aims to do this. The world of film, in theory, discussed in this book is both a pre-history for our present, but also

[32] Judith Williamson, personal interview, 26 February 2024. See also Judith Williamson, *Decoding Advertisements* (London: Marion Boyars, 1978).

a reminder of the progressive, vanguardist intellectual work which a cultural institution, and those who work with it, can undertake. It shows us how such compelling, transnational, intellectually challenging, consciousness-raising, even performatively stylish work can surge up through the institution's support and encouragement and challenge the political realities of our contemporary moment. The will to change provides this work with its attraction. It is important to end on a note of positivity: the work of BFI Education and *Screen* should continue to fascinate and inspire us as their utopian moment was faced with much of the same dangers and turmoil of the presence. These utopian desires are not repressed easily and can be revitalised in new forms and practices, often in the most unpredictable ways.

***

# Bibliography

For the most immediate accounts of this period, there is no better substitution than reading *Screen* journal, *Screen Education*, and *Sight & Sound*. All of the relevant articles from these publications are quoted within the main text. *Screen* journal is available to read in its entirety from Oxford Academic: https://academic.oup.com/screen/issue.

There is also an excellent collection of BFI-related materials at the Bill Douglas Cinema Museum, University of Exeter. Most of my archival research was conducted here.

Althusser, Louis, *Le lire capital*. Paris: François Maspero, 1965.

Althusser, Louis, 'Ideologie et appareils idéologiques d'État (notes pour une recherche)', *La Pensée* 151 (1970): 3–38.

Althusser, Louis, 'Freud and Lacan', trans. Ben Brewster, *New Left Review* 1, no. 55 (May–June 1969): 64–5.

Althusser, Louis, *Reading Capital*, trans. Ben Brewster. London: New Left Books, 1970.

Althusser, Louis, *For Marx*, trans. Ben Brewster. London: New Left Books, 1971.

Althusser, Louis, *Lenin and Philosophy and Other Essays*, trans. Ben Brewster. London: New Left Books, 1970.

Althusser, Louis, Etienne Balibar, Roger Establet, Pierre Macherey and Jacques Rancière, *Reading Capital: The Complete Edition*, trans. Ben Brewster and David Fernbach. London: Verso, 2015.

Anderson, Perry, *Arguments within English Marxism*. London: New Left Books, 1979.

Anderson, Perry, *Considerations on Western Marxism*. London: New Left Books, 1974.

Anderson, Perry, 'Conversations with History', https://www.youtube.com/watch?v=jjTKsRfVM9Q (accessed 31 August 2019).

Anderson, Perry, 'Diary', *London Review of Books* (21 October 1993): 24–5.

Anderson, Perry, *English Questions*. London: Verso, 1992.

Anderson, Perry, 'Ukania Perpetua', *New Left Review* 2, no. 125 (September–October 2020): 35–107.

Arnold, Matthew, *Culture and Anarchy*. Oxford: Oxford University Press, 2006.

'The Avignon Papers', Series 6/1, 1974, *Screen* Archive, University of Glasgow.

'BFI Education Seminars', BFI Education Seminar Papers, Bill Douglas/Peter Jewell Collection, Bill Douglas Cinema Museum, University of Exeter, 1967–70.

Bann, Stephen, ed., *Form*, 7 (March 1968).

Barry, Andrew, Thomas Osborne and Nikolas Rose, eds, *Foucault and Political Reason: Liberalism, Neo-Liberalism, and Rationalities of Government*. London: University College London, 1997.

Bazalgette, Cary, ed., *Report of the Commission of Inquiry into English: Balancing Literature, Language and Media in the National Curriculum*. London: BFI, 1994.

Berger, John, and Jean Mohr, *A Fortunate Man*. London: Penguin/Allen Lane, 1967.

Barr, Charles, *A Very Short Introduction to British Cinema*. Oxford: Oxford University Press, 2023.

Barthes, Roland, *S/Z*. Paris: Editions du Seuil, 1970.

Barthes, Roland, *S/Z*, trans. Richard Miller. New York: Farrar, Straus & Giroux, 1974.

Barthes, Roland, *The Pleasure of the Text*, trans. Richard Miller. New York: Farrar, Straus & Giroux, 1975.

Barthes, Roland, *Sade, Fourier, Loyola*, trans. Richard Miller. New York: Hill & Wang, 1975.

Barthes, Roland, *Image-Music-Text*, trans. Stephen Heath. London: Fontana, 1977.

Bolas, Terry, *Screen Education: From Film Appreciation to Media Studies*. Bristol: Intellect, 2009.

Bordwell, David, *Post-Theory: Reconstructing Film Studies*. Madison: University of Wisconsin Press, 1996.

Bradbury, Malcolm, 'Terminal Sex', *The Observer*, 1 April 1984.

Bradbury, Malcolm, *Mensonge: My Strange Quest for Structuralism's Hidden Hero*. London: HarperCollins, 1987.

Brewster, Ben, 'Presentation of Althusser', *New Left Review* 1, no. 41 (January–February 1967): 14.

Brewster, Ben, 'Comment', *New Left Review* 1, no. 77 (May–June 1969): 70–3.

Brewster, Ben, 'Communication on Ceylon and China', *New Left Review* 1, no. 70 (November–December 1971): 111.

'A Brief History of the New Left Review, 1960-2010', https://newleftreview.org/pages/history (accessed 18 January 2021).

Brophy, Brigid, 'James Joyce and the Reader's Understanding', *London Review of Books* 2, no. 3 (21 February 1980); reprinted in *The Meaninglessness of Meaning: Writing about the Theory Wars from the* London Review of Books (London: LRB Collections, 2020).

Buckland, Warren, 'La Politique des Auteurs in British Film Studies: Traditional versus Structural Approaches', *Mise au point* [En ligne], http://journals.openedition.org/map/2014 (accessed 12 April 2021).

Butler, Ivan, *To Encourage the Art of Film: The Story of the British Film Institute.* London: Hale, 1971.

Butt, Gavin, Kodwo Eshun, Mark Fisher, eds, *Post-Punk Then and Now.* London: Repeater, 2016.

Carroll, David, ed., *The States of 'Theory': History, Art, and Critical Discourse.* New York: Columbia University Press, 1990.

Caughie, John, ed., *Theories of Authorship.* London: BFI, 1981.

Commission on Educational and Cultural Films, *The Film in National Life.* London: George Allen & Unwin, 1932.

Coward, Rosalind, and John Ellis, *Language and Materialism: Development in Semiology and the Theory.* London: Routledge, 1977.

Cusset, Francois, *French Theory: How Foucault, Derrida, Deleuze, & Co. Transformed the Intellectual Life of the United States.* Minneapolis: University of Minnesota Press, 2004.

Derrida, Jacques, *La Voix et le phénomène.* Paris, P.U.F., Collection, 1967.

Derrida, Jacques, *L'Écriture et la différence.* Paris, Seuil, 1967.

Derrida, Jacques, *De la grammatologie.* Paris: Éditions de Minuit, 1967.

Derrida, Jacques, *Of Grammatology*, trans. Gayati Chakravorty Spivak. Baltimore: Johns Hopkins University Press, 1976/1998.

Derrida, Jacques, *Writing and Difference*, trans. Alan Bass. Chicago: University of Chicago Press, 1978.

Dibb, Mike (dir.), *Personally Speaking: A Long Conversation with Stuart Hall.* Northampton, MA: Media Education Foundation DVD, 2009.

Dumont, Lucile, 'The Moving Frontiers of Intellectual Work: The Importation and Early Reception of Roland Barthes' Work in the United States (1960s–1980s)', *Sociologica*, 2017), doi.10.2383/86984, 1–45.

Eagleton, Terry, 'Aesthetics and Politics', *New Left Review* 1, no. 107 (January–February 1978): 23.

Eckert, Charles W., 'The English Cine-Structuralists', *Film Comment* 9, no. 3 (1973): 47.

Elliott, Gregory, 'Louis Pierre Althusser Obituary', *Radical Philosophy* 57 (Spring 1991): 28–30.

Elliott, Gregory, *Perry Anderson: The Merciless Laboratory of History.* Minneapolis: University of Minnesota Press, 1998.

'Emancipation in the Heart of Darkness: An Interview with Juliet Mitchell', *The Platypus Review* 38 (August 2011), https://platypus1917.org/wp/content/uploads/2011/08/38/Singh/Mitchell1.pdf (accessed 12 December 2019).

Fabian, Rachel, 'Reconsidering the Work of Claire Johnston', *Feminist Media Histories* 4, no. 3 (Summer 2018): 244–73.

Ffrench, Patrick, *The Time of Theory: History of 'Tel Quel', 1960-83.* Oxford: Clarendon Press, 1995.

*Film Teaching.* London; BFI Education Department, 1964.

Foucault, Michel, *The Archaeology of Knowledge.* London: Tavistock, 1972.

Foucault, Michel, *Discipline and Punish.* New York: Random House, 1977.

Foucault, Michel, *History of Sexuality Volume 1: An Introduction.* London: Allen Lane, 1979.

*Ghost Times.* Essex: University of Essex, 1975.

Gibbs, John, 'Interviews: Ian Cameron, V.F. Perkins, Charles Barr, Alan Lovell', *Movie: A Journal of Film Criticism* 8 (2019), http://centaur.reading.ac.uk/84433/ (accessed 1 May 2020.

Go, Julian, and Monica Krause, eds, *Fielding Transnationalism.* London: Goldsmiths Press, 2016.

Goldmann, Lucien, *The Hidden God: A Study of Tragic Vision in the Pensées of Pascal and the Tragedies of Racine.* London: Routledge, 1964.

Green, Matthew, 'Coffee in a Coffin: The Fascinating Story of Le Macabre – and Soho's 1950s Espresso Revolution', *The Daily Telegraph*, 9 March 2017, https://www.telegraph.co.uk/travel/destinations/europe/united/kingdom/england/london/articles/the/amazing/story/of/soho/1950s/espresso/revolution/ (accessed 18 January 2021).

Grievson, Lee, and Haidee Wasson, eds, *Inventing Film Studies.* Durham. Duke University Press, 2008.

Griffith, Clark, *The Long Shadow: Emily Dickinson's Tragic Poetry.* Princeton: Princeton University Press, 1964.

Guilbaut, Serge, and Scott Watson, 'From an Interview with Peter Wollen', http://www.belkin.ubc.ca/_archived/lastcall/current/page1.html (accessed 4 May 2020).

Hall, Stuart, 'The Emergence of Cultural Studies and the Crisis of the Humanities', *October* 53, The Humanities as Social Technology (Summer, 1990): 11–23.

Hall, Stuart, 'Editorial', *New Left Review* 1, no. 1 (January–February 1960): 5.

Hall, Stuart, 'Life and Times of the First New Left', *New Left Review* 2, no. 61 (January–February 2010): 8.

Hall, Stuart, Dorothy Hobson, Andrew Lowe and Paul Wills, eds, *Culture, Media and Language: Working Papers in Cultural Studies 1972–79.* London: Routledge, 1981.

Hall, Stuart, with Bill Schwarz, *Familiar Stranger.* London: Allen Lane, 2017.

Halliday Jon, and Douglas Sirk, *Sirk on Sirk.* London: BFI/Secker and Warburg, 1971.

Heath, Stephen, Colin MacCabe and Christopher Prendergast, eds, *Signs of the Times: Introductory Readings in Textual Semiotics.* Cambridge: Instaprint, n.d.

Helm-Grovas, Nicolas, Laura Mulvey and Peter Wollen 1963-1983: Theory and Practice, Aesthetics and Politics, unpublished PhD thesis, Royal Holloway, University of London, 2018.

Hewison, Robert, *Culture and Consensus: England, art and politics since 1940*. London: Methuen, 1995.

Hills, Janet, *Are They Safe at the Cinema? A Considered Answer to Critics of the Cinema*. London: BFI, 1953.

Hindess, Barry, and Paul Hirst, *Mode of Production and Social Formation: An Auto-Critique of Pre-Capitalist Modes of Production* London: Palgrave Macmillan, 1977.

Hoare, Quintin, 'On Juliet Mitchell's Women: The Longest Revolution', *New Left Review* 1, no. 41 (January–February 1967): 80.

Hollows, Joanne, and Mark Jancovic, *Approaches to Popular Film*. New York: Manchester University Press, 1995.

Horowitz, Daniel, *Consuming Pleasures: Intellectuals and Popular Culture in the Postwar World*. Pennsylvania: University of Pennsylvania Press, 2012.

Houston, Penelope, 'The Critical Question', *Sight and Sound* 29, no. 4 (Autumn 1960): 160–5.

Hunter, I. Q., Laraine Porter and Justin Smith eds, *The Routledge Companion to British Cinema History*. London: Routledge, 2017.

Jackson, Lauren Michele, 'The Invention of the Male Gaze', *New Yorker*, 14 July 2023, https://www.newyorker.com/books/second-read/the-invention-of-the-male-gaze (accessed 2 June 2024).

Jardine, Lisa, and Julia Swindells, *What's Left? Women In Culture and the Labour Movement*. London: Routledge, 1990.

Johnson, Richard, and Stuart Hall, eds, *Culture, Media Language: Working Papers in Cultural Studies*. Birmingham: University of Birmingham, 1980.

Johnston, Claire, and Paul Willemen, eds, *Jacques Tourneur*. Edinburgh: Edinburgh Film Festival, 1975.

Johnston, Claire ed., *Notes on Women's Cinema*. London: BFI, 1973.

Kaminsky, Stuart and Gerald Peary, "Structuralism implies a certain kind of methodology…", *Film Heritage* 9:4 (Fall 1974).

Kaplan, E. Ann, ed., *Woman in Film Noir*. London: BFI, 1980.

Kelly, Mary, 'A Secret Agreement: An Era Defined by the Events of 1968', https://www.tate.org.uk/whats-on/tate-modern/talk/mary-kelly-conversation-hans-ulrich-obrist/secret-agreement-era-defined (accessed 25 May 2021).

Kenny, Michael, *The First New Left: British Intellectuals after Stalin*. London: Lawrence and Wishart, 1995.

Kitses, Jim, *Horizons West*. London: BFI, 1967.

Lacan, Jacques, *Écrits: A Selection*. London: Tavistock, 1977.

Lapsley, Robert, and Kevin Westlake, *Film Theory: An Introduction*. Manchester: Manchester University Press, 1988.

Leavis, F. R., *Education and the University: A Sketch for an 'English School'*. London: Chatto and Windus, 1948.

Leavis, F. R., *Mass Civilisation and Minoriy Culture*. Cambridge: Minority Press, 1930.

Leavis, F. R., and Denys Thompson, *Culture and Environment*. London: Chatto and Windus, 1962.

Lejeune, Anael, Olivier Mignon and Raphael Pirenne eds, *French Theory and American Art*. Berlin: Sternberg Press, 2013.

'Letter from B. Ruby Rich', Series 6/12, 22 May 1983, *Screen* Archive, University of Glasgow.

Lévi-Strauss, Claude, *La Pensée sauvage*. Paris: Librarie Plon, 1962.

Lévi-Strauss, Claude, *The Savage Mind*. London: Weidenfield and Nicolson 1966.

Lévi-Strauss, Claude, *Wild Thoughts*. Chicago: University of Chicago Press, 2021.

Lindgren, Ernest, *Art of the Film*. London: Allen and Unwin, 1948.

Lovell, Alan, 'Appreciation: Paddy Whannel 1922-1980', *BFI News* 45 (October 1980).

Lusted, David, ed., *Guide to Film Studies in Secondary and Further Education*. London: BFI Education, 1983.

MacArthur, Colin, 'Two Steps Forward, One Step Back: Cultural Struggle in the BFI', ed. James Chapman and Christine Geraghty, *Journal of Popular British Cinema* 4 (2001), 112–27.

MacCabe, Colin, 'The Future of Screen', Series 6/6, 14 May 1979, *Screen* Archive, University of Glasgow.

MacCabe, Colin, 'Notes on Possible Brecht Event', Series 6/1, 17 October 1974, *Screen* Archive, University of Glasgow.

MacCabe, Colin, *On the Eloquence of the Vulgar: Justification of the Study of Film and Television*. London: BFI, 1993.

MacCabe, Colin, *Tracking the Signifier: Theoretical Essays: Film, Linguistics, Literature*. Manchester: Manchester University Press, 1985.

MacDonald, Richard Lowell, *The Appreciation of Film: The Postwar Film Society Movement and Film Culture in Britain*. Exeter: University of Exeter Press, 2016.

MacGowan, Todd, *Psychoanalytic Film Theory and the Rules of the Game*. London: Bloomsbury, 2015.

McNamee, Robert V, 'Writing for Film: The Role of the Production Board of the British Film Institute', unpublished DPhil thesis, University of Oxford, https://ora.ox.ac.uk/objects/uuid:bf4bcf2d/4120/4c59/a196/05d9f771a9dc (accessed 28 April 2020).

Manvell, Roger, *Film*. London: Pelican, 1944.

Manvell, Roger, *The Film and the Public*. London: Pelican, 1955.

Marchant, James, *The Cinema in Education: Being the Report of the Psychological Investigation Conducted by Special Subcommittees Appointed by the Cinema*

*Commission of Enquiry Established by the National Council of Public Morals.* London: Allen & Unwin, 1925.

Martin, Adrian, '[Review of] *Paris Hollywood*', http://www.filmcritic.com.au/essays/book_paris.html (accessed 5 May 2020).

Martin, Adrian, 'Sam Rohdie', http://www.filmcritic.com.au/essays/rohdie.html (accessed 10 August 2020).

Marx-Scouras, Danielle, 'The Dissident Politics of "Tel Quel"', Literature of Change, Opposition & Revolution, *L'Esprit Créateur* 27, no. 2 (Summer 1987): 101–8.

Marx-Scouras, Danielle, *The Cultural Politics of Tel Quel: Literature and the Left in the Wake of Engagement*. Pennsylvania: University of Pennsylvania Press, 1996.

Masschelein, Anneleen, 'Ways of Seeing/Ways of Talking: Conversation and Collage in the Films of Mike Dibb', Franklin, Cynthia, Craig Howes, John Zuern and Anna Poletti, eds, *Biography* 41, no. 2 (Spring 2018): 344–60.

Matthews, Peter, 'Diving the Real: The Leaps of Faith in André Bazin's Film Criticism', https://www2.bfi.org.uk/news-opinion/sight-sound-magazine/features/andre-bazin-divining-real-film-criticism-overview (accessed 10 June 2024).

Merck, Mandy, 'Mulvey's Manifesto', *Camera Obscura* 66, 22, no. 3 (2007): 1–22.

Merck, Mandy, ed., *The Sexual Subject: A Screen Reader in Sexuality*. London: Routledge, 1992.

Metz, Christian, *Film Language: A Semiotics of the Cinema*. Oxford: Oxford University Press, 1975.

Metz, Christian, 'Le signifiant imaginaire', *Communications* 23 (1975): 3–55.

Miles, Barry, *London Calling*. London: Atlantic Books, 2011.

Miller, Henry K., 'The Slade School and Cinema', *Vertigo Magazine* 3, no. 5 (2007).

Miller, Jonathan, 'Anatomy of Pop Culture', *The Guardian*, 13 December 1964.

Millot, Catherine *Hors-sexe*. Paris: Point Hors Ligne, 1983.

Mitchell, Juliet, 'Women: the Longest Revolution', *New Left Review* 1, no. 40 (November–December 1966): 10–37.

Mitchell, Juliet, 'Juliet Mitchell: Looking Back at Woman's Estate', https://www.versobooks.com/blogs/1836/juliet/mitchell/looking/back/at/woman/s/estate (accessed 20 January 2020).

Mulvey, Laura, 'You Don't Know What Is Happening, Do You, Mr. Jones?', *Spare Rib* 8 (February 1973): 13–30.

Mulvey, Laura, 'The Hole Truth', *Spare Rib* 17 (November 1973): 37.

Nobus, Dany, 'The Irredeemable Debt: On the English Translation of Lacan's First Two Public Seminars', *Psychoanalysis and History* 19, no. 2 (2017): 173–212.

Nowell-Smith, Geoffrey, and Christophe Dupin, eds, *The British Film Institute, the Government and Film Culture, 1933–2000*. Manchester: Manchester University Press, 2012.

'On the Passage of a Few People through a Rather Brief Period of Time', https://www.tate.org.uk/documents/999/on_the_passage_of_a_few_people_through_a_rather_brief_period_of_time.pdf (accessed 10 June 2024).

O'Pray, Michael, *The British Avant-Garde Film 1926–1995*. Luton: University of Luton Press, 1995.

Pater, Walter, *Appreciations, with an Essay on Style*. London: Macmillan, 1889.

Paterson, Richard, 'In Memory of Anthony Smith CBE, Former Director of the BFI and BFI Fellow, 1938 to 2021', https://www.bfi.org.uk/news/anthony-smith-cbe-1938-2021-director-bfi (accessed 10 June 2024).

'Peter Wollen Obituary: A Prophet of Film Theory', https://twitter.com/bfi/status/1209046748439683073?lang=en (accessed 12 April 2021).

Pines, Jim, *Blacks in the Cinema: The Changing Image*. London: BFI Education, 1971.

Pines, Jim, *Blacks in Films*. London: Studio Vista, 1975.

Pye, Douglas, ed., *V. F. Perkins on Movies*. Detroit: Wayne State University Press, 2020.

*Report of the Review Committee of Educational Services*, mimeographed report. London: BFI, 1970.

Rhode, Eric, 'The British Cinema in the Seventies', *The Listener* 82, no. 2107 (1969): 201.

Rodowick, D. N., *The Crisis of Political Modernism: Criticism and Ideology in Contemporary Film Theory*. Berkeley: University of California Press, 1994.

'The Russell Harty Show', London Weekend Television, 21 September 1978.

Sarris, Andrew, 'Notes on the Auteur Theory in 1962', *Film Culture* 27 (Winter 1962–3): 1–8.

'Screen Minutes and Accompanying Documents, 1980', Series 6/7, *Screen* Archive, University of Glasgow.

Smith, Henry Nash, *Virgin Land: The American West as Symbol and Myth*. Cambridge, MA: Harvard University Press, 1950.

'Suddenly, a Woman Spectator: An Interview with Laura Mulvey', *Another Gaze*, https://www.anothergaze.com/suddenly-woman-spectator-conversation-interview-feminism-laura-mulvey/ (accessed 28 May 2021).

Thompson, E. P., *The Peculiarities of the English*. London: Socialist Register, 1965. Reprinted in *The Poverty of Theory*. London: Merlin, 1978.

Thorpe, Vanessa, 'How a Soho Coffee-House Gave Birth to The New Left', *The Guardian*, 23 April 2017, https://www.theguardian.com/politics/2017/apr/22/cafe-cnd-new-left (accessed 18 January 2021).

Tickner, Lisa, *London's New Scene: Art and Culture in the 1960s*. London: Paul Mellon Centre, 2020.

Tredell, Nicolas, ed., *Conversations with Critics*. London: Sheep Meadow Press, 1994.

Tudor, Andrew, *Theories of Film*. London: Secker and Warburg, 1974.

Wasson, Haidee, *Museum Movies: The Museum of Modern Art and the Birth of Art Cinema*. Berkeley: University of California Press, 2005.

Whannel, Paddy, 'Letter to Eric Rhode', 1970, Nicky North/Paddy Whannel Files, BFI Archive Box 91.

Whannel, Paddy, 'The State of Film Culture', internal BFI memo, 4 December 1968, BFI Archive, Nicky North/Paddy Whannel files, Box 91.

Whannel, Paddy, 'Towards a Positive Criticism of the Mass Media', *Film Teacher* (17 May 1959): 28–30.

Whannel, Paddy, and Brian Groombridge, 'Something Rotten in Denmark Street', *New Left Review* 1, no. 1 (January–February 1960): 52–4.

Whannel, Paddy, and Stuart Hall, *The Popular Arts*, first edition. London: Hutchinson Education, 1964.

Whannel, Paddy, and Stuart Hall, *The Popular Arts*. Durham: Duke University Press, 2018.

Widgery, David, ed., *The Left in Britain, 1956-1968*. Harmondsworth: Penguin, 1976.

Williamson, Judith, *Decoding Advertisements*. London: Marion Boyars, 1978.

Williamson, Judith, 'Viewfinder', *New Statesman*, 12 December 1986.

Wieland, Justus, *Happiness by Design*. Minneapolis: University of Minnesota Press, 2020.

Wigley, Samuel, 'Looking for Signs and Meaning in the Cinema', https://www2.bfi.org.uk/news-opinion/news-bfi/interviews/looking-signs-meaning-cinema (accessed 26 May 2021).

Williams, Deane, 'Some Things You Never Learn: An Interview with Sam Rohdie', http://www.Screeningthepast.com/issue-28-australian-film-culture-australian-research-council-interviews/some-things-you-never-learn/ (accessed 10 June 2024).

Williams, Raymond, *Culture and Society, 1780–1950*. Harmondsworth: Penguin, 1958.

Williams, Raymond, *Politics and Letters: Interviews With New Left Review*. London: Verso, 2015.

Williams, Raymond, *Resources of Hope: Culture, Democracy, Socialism*. London: Verso, 1989.

Wilson, Siona, *Art Labor, Sex Politics: Feminist Effects in 1970s British Art and Performance*. Minneapolis: University of Minnesota Press, 2015.

Wollen, Peter, 'Cinema and Semiology', Form 7 (March 1968): 9–15.

Wollen, Peter, [as Lee Russell], 'Culture and Cinema', *New Left Review* 1, no. 21 (September–October 1963): 112–14.

Wollen, Peter, [as L. R.], 'The Long Shadow', *New Left Review* 1, no. 25 (May–June 1964): 94.

Wollen, Peter, [as Lee Russell], 'Samuel Fuller', *New Left Review* 1, no. 23 (January–February 1964): 86–9.

Wollen, Peter, 'The Avant-Gardes: Europe and America', *Framework: The Journal of Cinema and Media* no. 14 (Spring 1981): 9–10.

Wollen, Peter, *Friendship's Death* [Film], BFI, 1987.

Wollen, Peter, 'Hitchcock's Vision', *Cinema* 1, no. 3 (June 1969): 2.

Wollen, Peter, 'Memo to Paddy Whannel', 4 August 1968, Nicky North/Paddy Whannel files, BFI Archive Box 91.

Wollen, Peter, *Signs and Meaning in the Cinema*. London: BFI, 1969.

Wollen, Peter, *Signs and Meaning in the Cinema*, fifth edition. London: BFI, 2013.

Wollen, Peter, 'Thinking Theory', *Film Comment* 24, no. 4 (July–August 1988): 50–1.

Wollen, Peter, 'The Two Avant-Gardes', *Studio International* (November–December 1975): 171–5.

Wollen, Peter, Untitled document, PWO 4-1, Peter Wollen Archive, British Film Institute.

Wood, Ellen Meiskins, 'A Chronology of the New Left and Its Successors, or: Who's Old-Fashioned Now?', *Socialist Register* (1995): 30–57.

# Index